To survivors everywhere—
You are not alone.

Contents

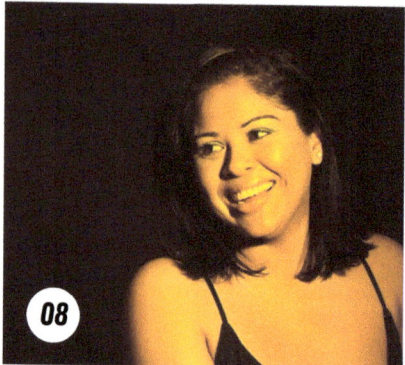
48

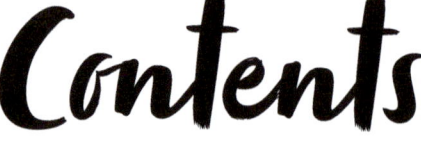
18

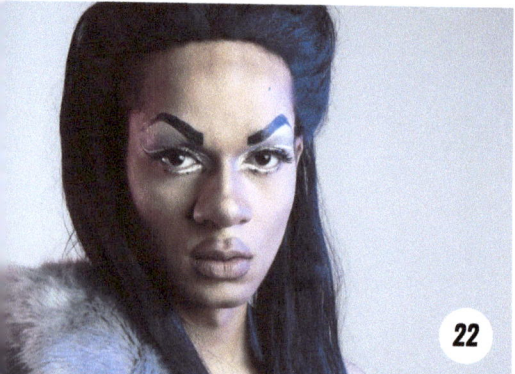
08

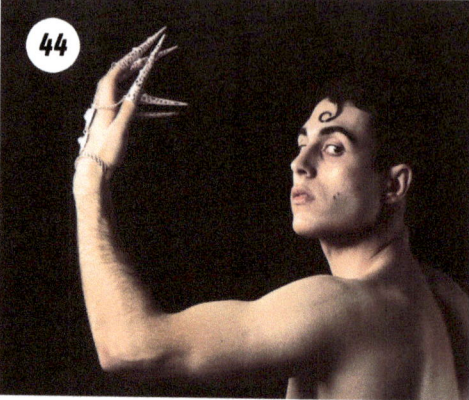
44

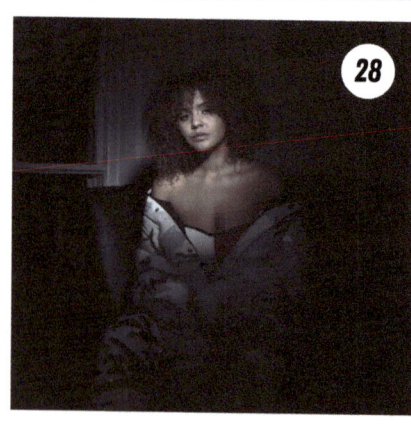
22

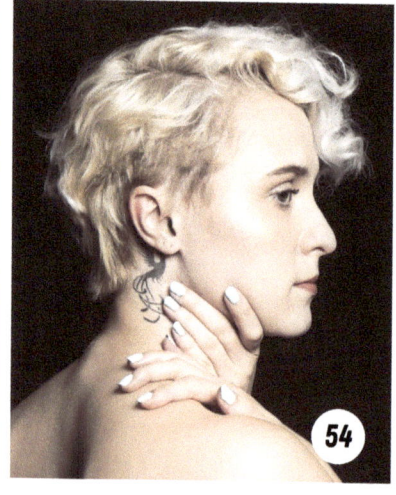
54

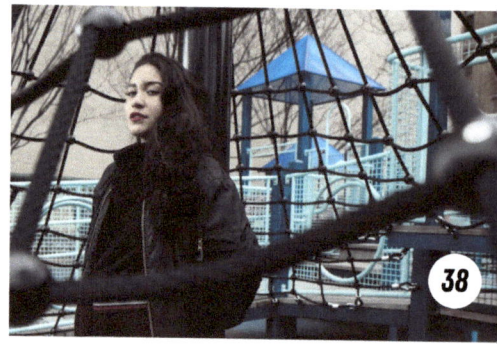
38

28

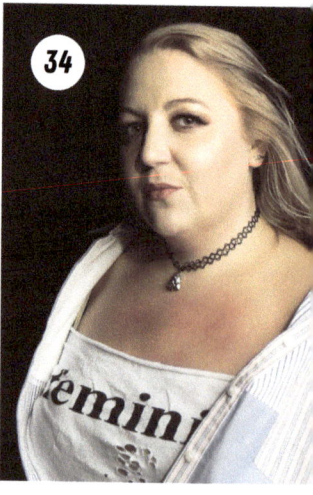
34

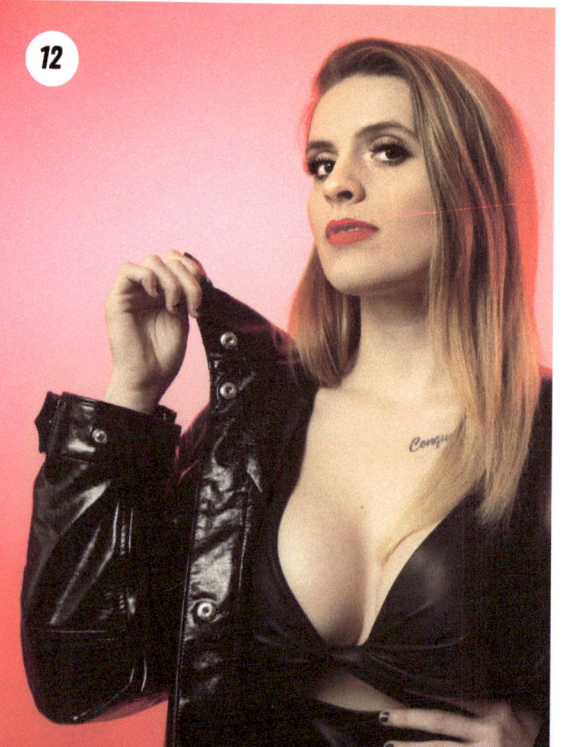
12

Letter from the Editor

I was going to begin this letter the way I begin many explanations of Survivors Magazine: with the story of my assault. I paused, however, when I realized that I've lost count of how many times I have shared my assault story. Since I began advocating on behalf of survivors, I have become an expert at packaging my assault into a story that the public will be able to swallow. At times, I believed my experience could be as simple as a couple of paragraphs. With the rise of movements like #MeToo and #TimesUp, we, consumers of American media, have seen more survivors take on the burden of packaging their stories to the public. If the survivor is not white and heterosexual, the story will likely remain in the margins. If the survivor does not spell out their own innocence, people might say they are lying.

The reality is that every survivor story is so much more than what we will read. I wish my experience could be as simple as a couple of paragraphs. I wish it were that simple because that might mean the solutions are simple, too. If the epidemic of sexual assault was as simple as not enough rapists going to jail, then we wouldn't have to deal with the fact our incarceration system produces more harm than good. If this epidemic was as simple as taking better precautions to protect ourselves, then we wouldn't have to deal with the fact that no amount of pepper spray can protect our teenagers from intimate partner rape. There is a lot of grey area in this national dialogue, but to be clear, survivors are always the experts in their own lives. And, ultimately, a survivor does not have to share their story at all for their identity as a survivor to be valid.

The fact that survivors endure violence on their bodies but continue to claim space with those same bodies is evidence enough of survivorship. Survivors persevere as poets, teachers, and doctors, as sex-workers, priests, and family members, and we—the public, their community, perhaps fellow survivors—do not need to know anything about an individual's assault to support them in taking on "survivor" as part of their identity, if that is how they choose to heal. It is necessary that as these national movements encourage survivors to share their stories, we do not make disclosure an expectation to enter the conversation.

The majority of the people in this magazine never disclosed details of their assault. It was not necessary to understand who they are as people and how we could make their vision come to life. My friend recently said to me, "I like this project because it's a project about survivors of sexual assault without really being about sexual assault." Survivors Magazine seeks to center survivors and their stories in a way that never asks them to relive their trauma. Part of that is due to the medium we are using: fashion and photography tell stories through metaphor, so survivors can get creative with how to emulate details they might otherwise not share. But a huge factor is thanks to the people involved: the creative team, the Alliance, and the survivors themselves strived to cultivate a space of honesty and trust every step of the way. To every participant, thank you for bringing the honesty of who you are to these pages. I hope our work together inspires others to continue making space for survivors to truly be the experts in their own lives.

Contributors

DIRECTOR
Maria Polzin
@survivorsnyc

PHOTOGRAPHER
Myles Golden
@mylesgolden

MAKEUP ARTIST
Chynna Walls
@chynnawalls

STYLISTS
Victor Leonard
@urthtoned

Nairobi Hilaire
@melanin.monro

ALLIANCE INTERVENTION COORDINATORS
Josie Torielli
LCSW, Assistant Director of Intervention Programs

Ashleigh Andersen
Direct Service Coordinator

LAYOUT DESIGNER
Lia Hagen
@lia_hagen

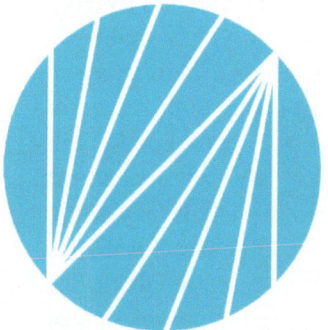

New York City Alliance Against Sexual Assault

The mission of the New York City Alliance Against Sexual Assault is to prevent sexual violence and reduce the harm it causes through education, advocacy and research. The Alliance was founded in 2000 by rape crisis centers in New York City in order to advocate for the needs of survivors and the programs that serve them. Through public education, cutting-edge programming, advocacy for survivors and the pursuit of legal and policy changes, the Alliance continues to expand as a hub for resources and information about sexual violence.

The Process

Sexual assault is an invasive assertion of power, and taking on the label of a "victim" unfortunately comes with so much negative judgement in today's rape culture. From the way the media addresses abuse to how our current president speaks about women to the small comments made by everyday people which seek to silence or shame, these circumstances can drastically complicate the victim's relationship with their identity and quickly cause them to feel out of control. How can one move on from sexual assault while allowing the experience to shape their identity? Furthermore, how can victims share their stories without bringing themselves down in the process? We started by calling victims "survivors" because claiming your experience should not be connoted with weakness. We then created a process that allows the survivors to be in control of the rest.

OUTREACH

Highly-trained intervention coordinators at The NYC Alliance Against Sexual Assault reach out to survivors over the age of 18 in the NYC area regarding their interest in participating in the publication. Survivors are also able to contact us directly should they hear of the project and want to partake. The individuals each go through a brief screening with a coordinator to ensure the individual's expectations of the experience are in line with what we can offer.

COLLABORATION

Once participants are identified, the creative team (photographer, makeup artist, creative consultants, and director) meet with the participant to get to know one another and build comfortability before the photoshoot itself. We work openly with the survivor to create a look that makes them feel confident and in control. Do they want to show a lot of skin or no skin? Makeup or no make up? Do they want to hold the photoshoot at a place of personal significance? Or incorporate items that are crucial to their healing process? Depending on the individual, the photos may have everything to do with sexual assault, or nothing at all, for each individual is so much more than the violences that stay with them.

PHOTOSHOOT

After meeting with the participant, we obtain all the resources needed to fulfill their vision. We then spend a full day doing their makeup (if desired) and photographing them. While it's normal for survivors to start off nervous, by the end of the shoot, partipants are confident in the identity they want to be claiming, and if they are not, that means the shoot is not over. We will toss ideas on the spot or work with something new until the survivor feels confident and in control.

CURATION

We send each partipant all of their photos, and they pick their favorites. The photographer edits 4 of their choices, and those are included in the magazine. Additionally, each survivor submits content for a personal page. The personal content can be anything that can be put onto pages — photographs, poetry, codes, comedy, drawings, paintings, and more. This allows the survivors to express themselves through a different medium.

Sexual Violence in America

Source: "30 Alarming Statistics That Show The Reality Of Sexual Violence In America" in the Huffington Post

---

EVERY 98 SECONDS

someone in the U.S. is sexually assaulted

570 people

in this country experience sexual violence in a single day

64

of trans people will experience sexual assault in their lifetimes

80,600 PEOPLE

who are incarcerated experience sexual violence in prison or jail every year

People with disabilities are 2

more likely to experience sexual assault than people without a disability

94

of survivors experience PTSD in the two weeks after the assault

On Consent

Source: "Everything You Need to Know About Consent That You Never Learned in Sex Ed" in Teen Vogue

Getting Enthusiastic Consent

Avoid partners who are vulnerable. When people are intoxicated, in a new situation, or acting recklessly, their ability to make decisions is compromised. If they are heavily intoxicated, unconscious, or not of legal age, they are not legally capable of providing consent.

Negotiate consent verbally. You can explicitly ask for permission, offer your partner something you'd like to do for them (ex: "I would love to kiss you"), or invite your partner to do something to you.

Establish "blanket consent" ahead of time by agreeing on an "only no means no" policy.

Negotiate consent nonverbally. Negotiating consent nonverbally is riskier, but there are some situations or partners where it is possible. As a general rule: build it up slowly, and get continued, reciprocated, and enthusiastic responses before you escalate to each subsequent intimate act.

Err on the side of caution. Be mindful.

Giving Enthusiastic Consent

Share your intentions and limitations. Don't assume that your partner wants what you want, or that they know what you want.

Let your partner what kind of consent works for you. Do you want your partner to check in with you frequently? Or would you prefer that they explore, and you will tell them if you are uncomfortable?

Provide continuous positive feedback. This can be anything from a "yes" or an "I like that" to nonverbal clues like touching your partner or returning kisses.

Get conmfortable saying "no" and learn to communicate it effectively. Saying no can be uncomfortable or difficult, but it is the clearest way to demonstrate how you're feeling.

Err on the side of caution. If you're not sure what you want, say no. You can always change your mind and say "yes" later.

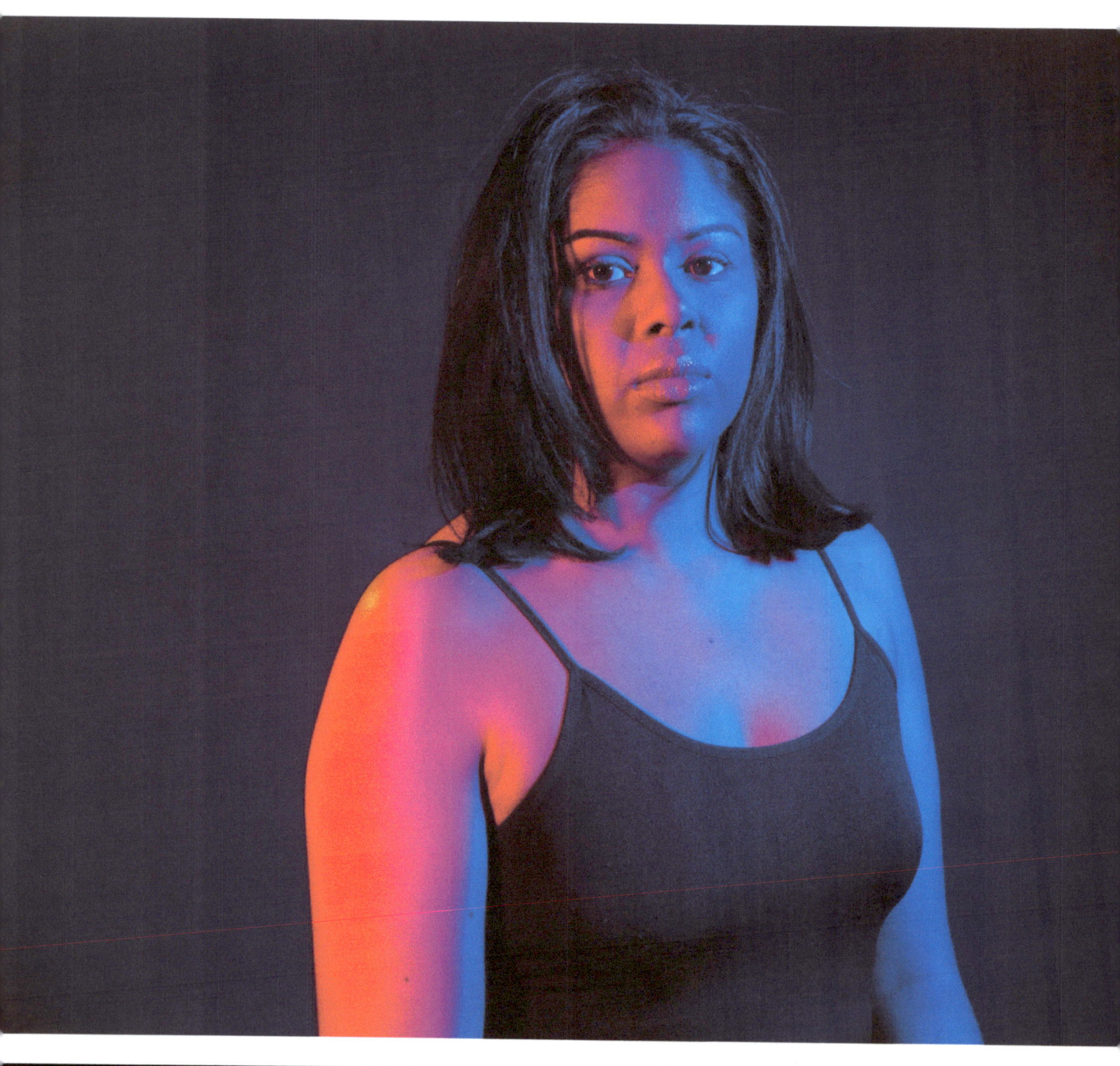

Rehanna Almestica

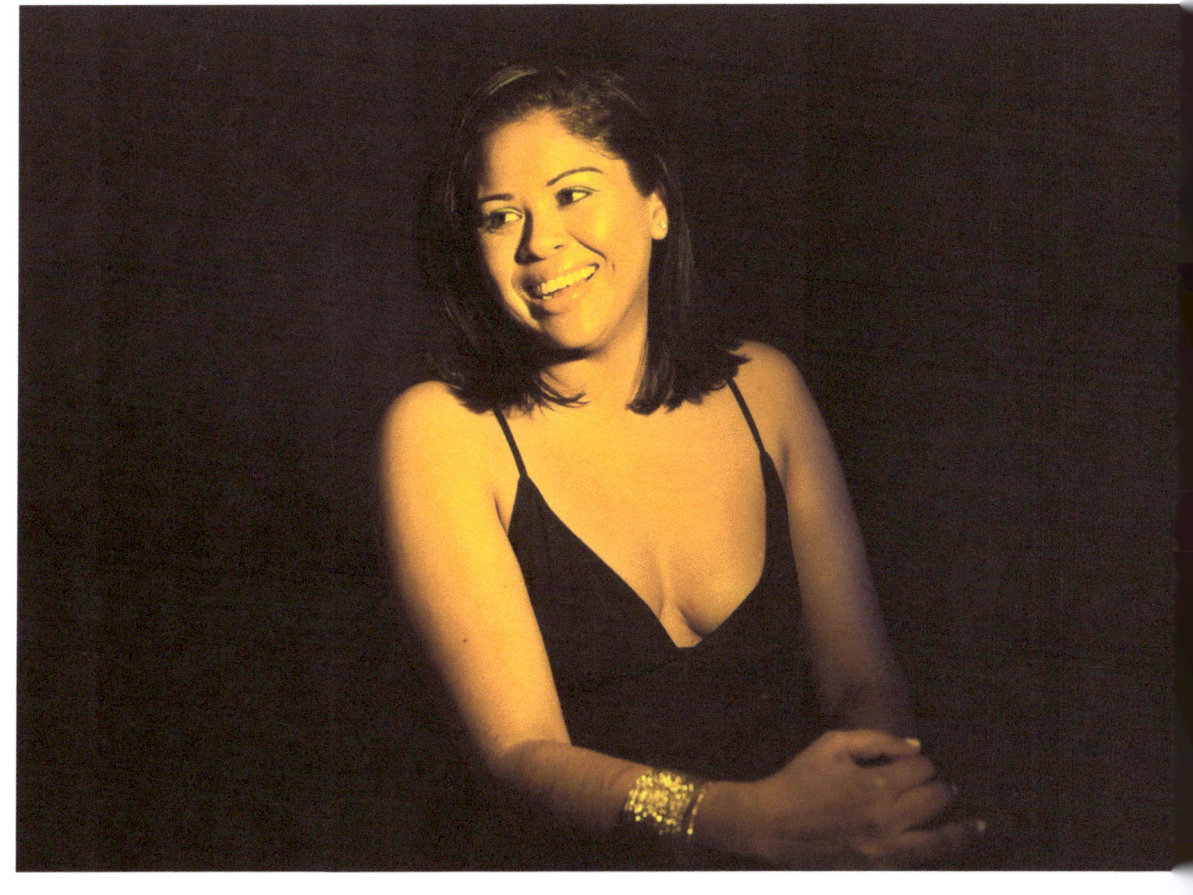

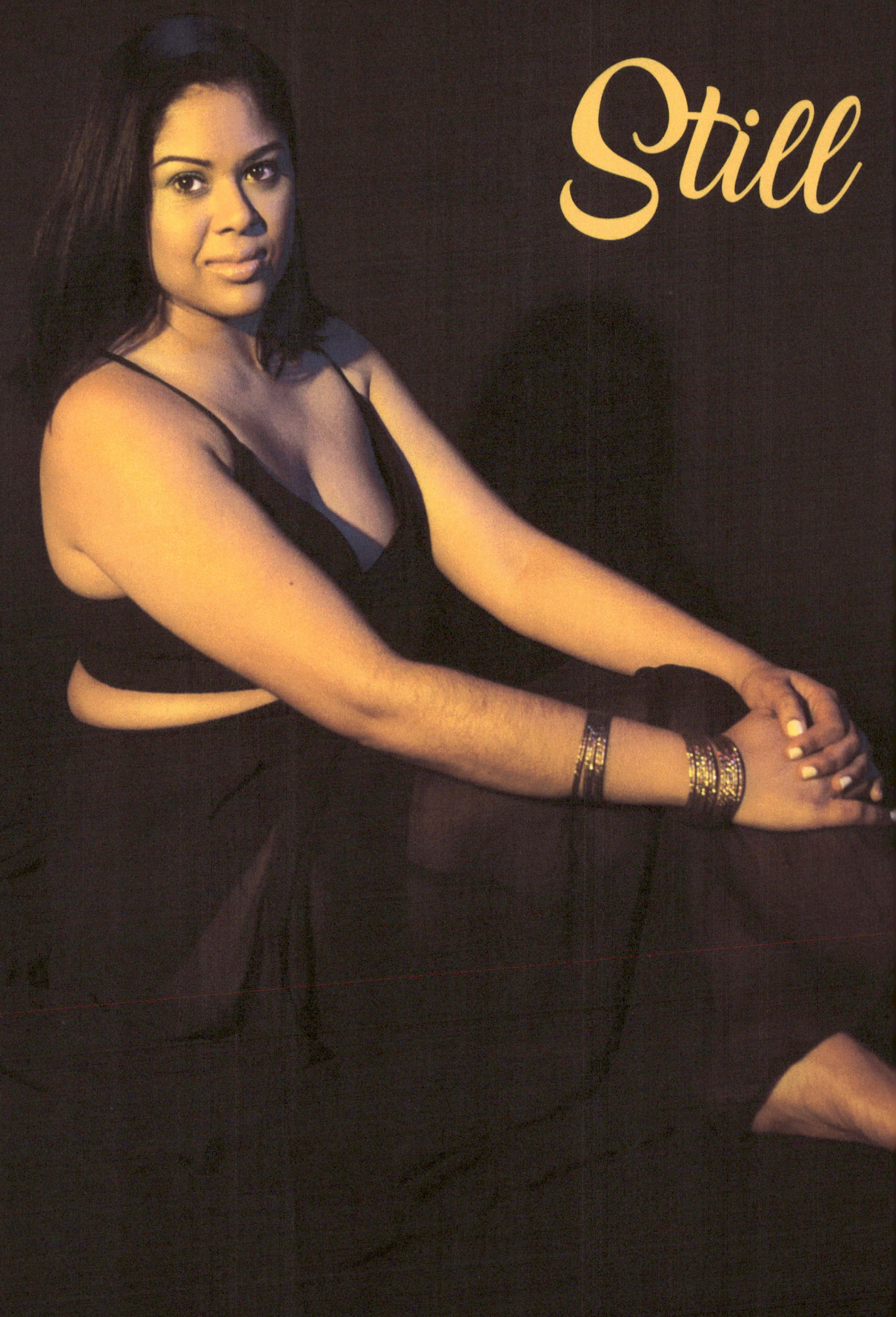

I Rise

I have decided to use Maya Angelou's Still I Rise as the piece to accompany my photos. She was someone I have admired since childhood, whose work and wisdom will always inspire me and sort of came full circle when I met her in 2008.

You may write me down in history
With your bitter, twisted lies,
You may trod me in the very dirt
But still, like dust, I'll rise.

Does my sassiness upset you?
Why are you beset with gloom?
'Cause I walk like I've got oil wells
Pumping in my living room.

Just like moons and like suns,
With the certainty of tides,
Just like hopes springing high,
Still I'll rise.

Did you want to see me broken?
Bowed head and lowered eyes?
Shoulders falling down like teardrops,
Weakened by my soulful cries?

Does my haughtiness offend you?
Don't you take it awful hard
'Cause I laugh like I've got gold mines
Diggin' in my own backyard.

You may shoot me with your words,
You may cut me with your eyes,
You may kill me with your hatefulness,
But still, like air, I'll rise.

Does my sexiness upset you?
Does it come as a surprise
That I dance like I've got diamonds
At the meeting of my thighs?

Out of the huts of history's shame
I rise
Up from a past that's rooted in pain
I rise
I'm a black ocean, leaping and wide,
Welling and swelling I bear in the tide.

Leaving behind nights of terror and fear
I rise
Into a daybreak that's wondrously clear
I rise
Bringing the gifts that my ancestors gave,
I am the dream and the hope of the slave.
I rise
I rise
I rise.

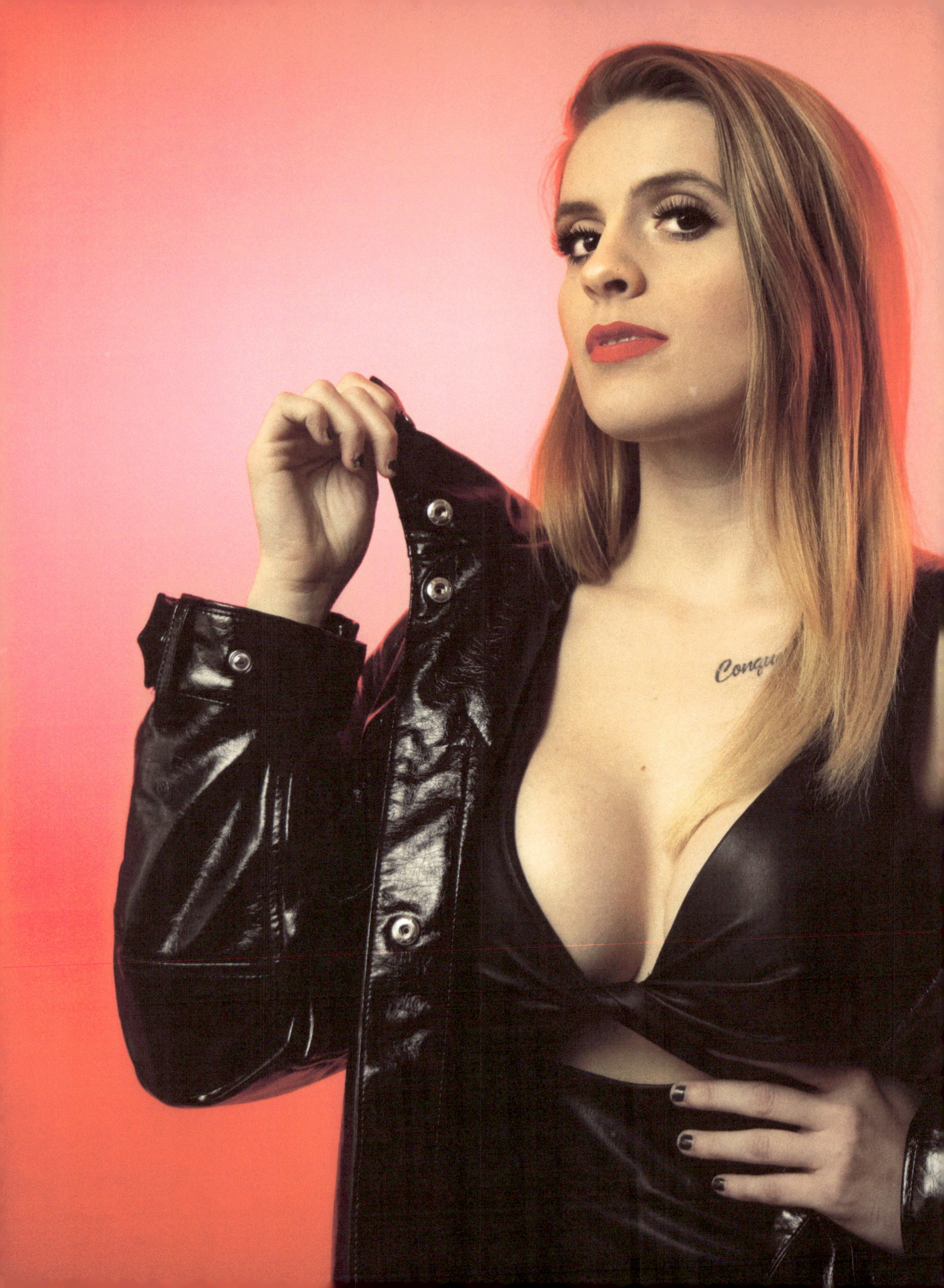

SAMANTHA McCOY

After the rape, I truly felt like I had lost all worth and confidence. This photoshoot allowed me to show a side that I didn't think I had anymore - a fierce, confident woman. It is the first time I have felt beautiful and worthy in my own skin. Healing is possible!

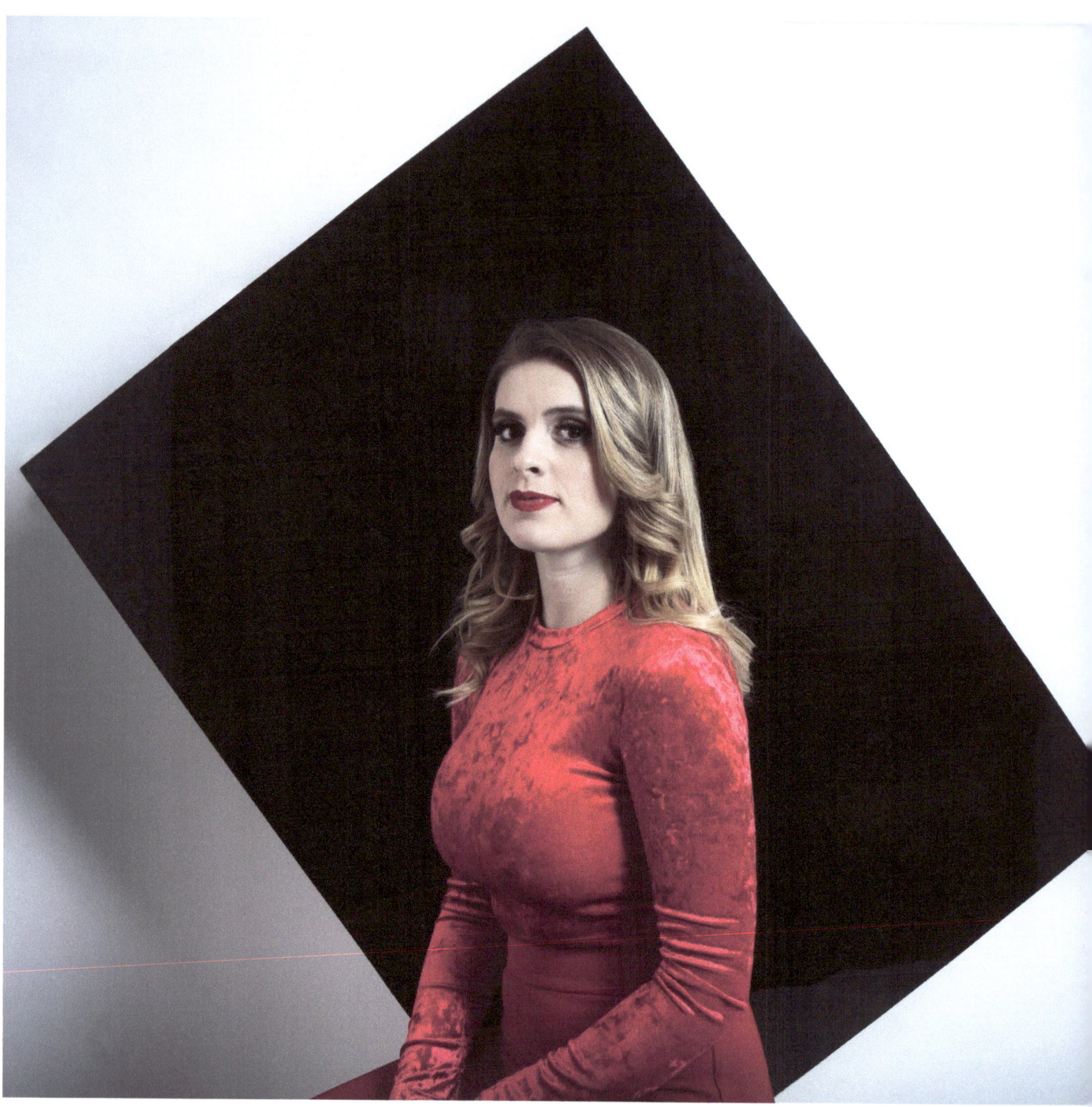

I WILL PREVAIL

You
Kind, gentle, warm
I had so much trust in you
You
Giving, passionate, loving
I felt invincible near you
You
Hidden lies, deceit, anger
It came so fast, I was thrown off track
You
Violence, rage, hate
No regard for the damage you had done to me
You
Rapist, offender, criminal
You stole my soul and my will to live that night
You
Coward, fake, poser
Never admitting the damage that you caused
You
Cocky, confident, arrogant
You will ruin another's life committing the same crime
You
Hateful, heartless, loner
You will be the one that becomes nothing in the end
You
Cannot hide from the truth forever
You
Will have to live with yourself and the consequences of your actions
You
No longer have control over me
I
Will rise above your evil
I
Will prevail.

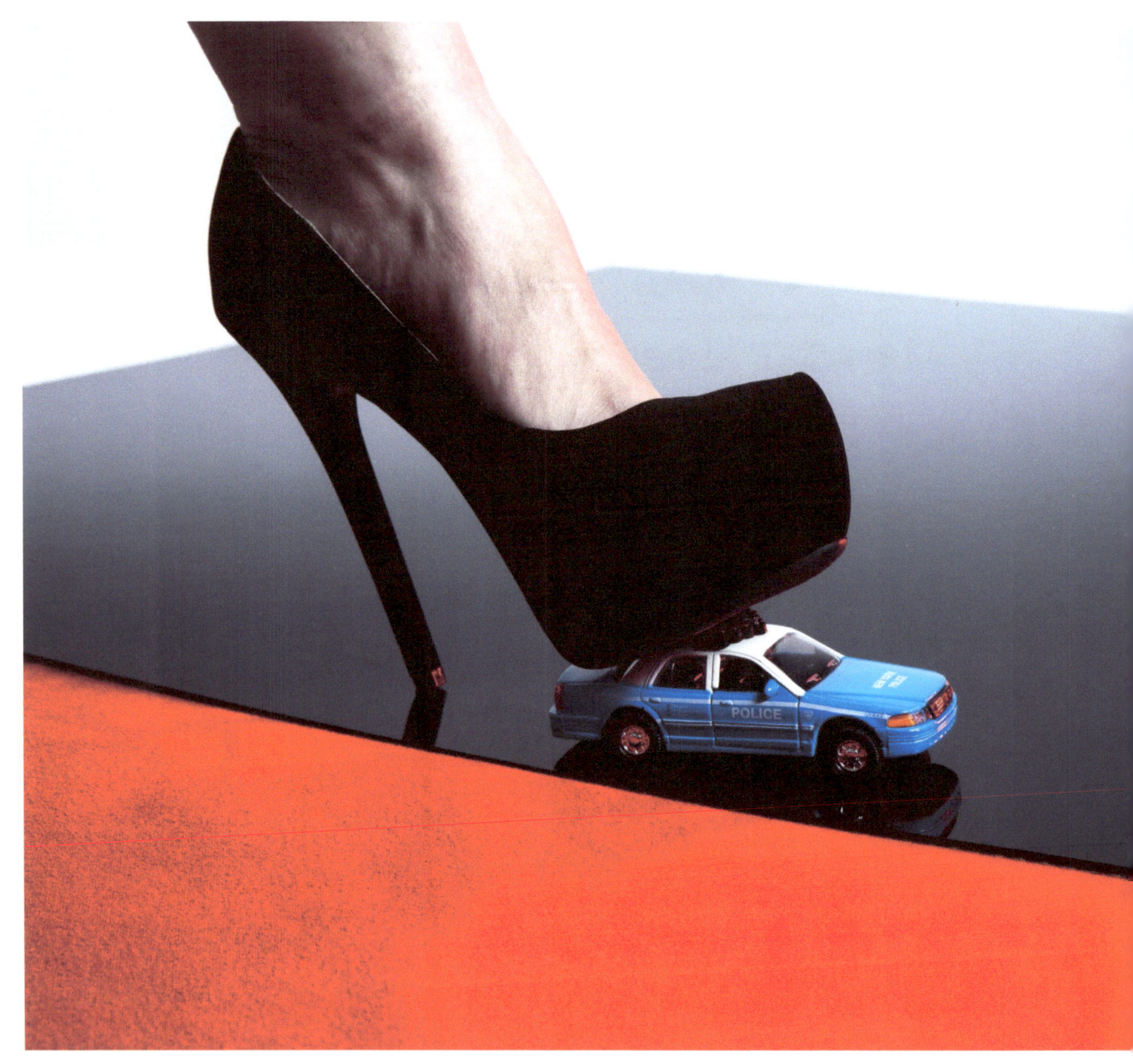

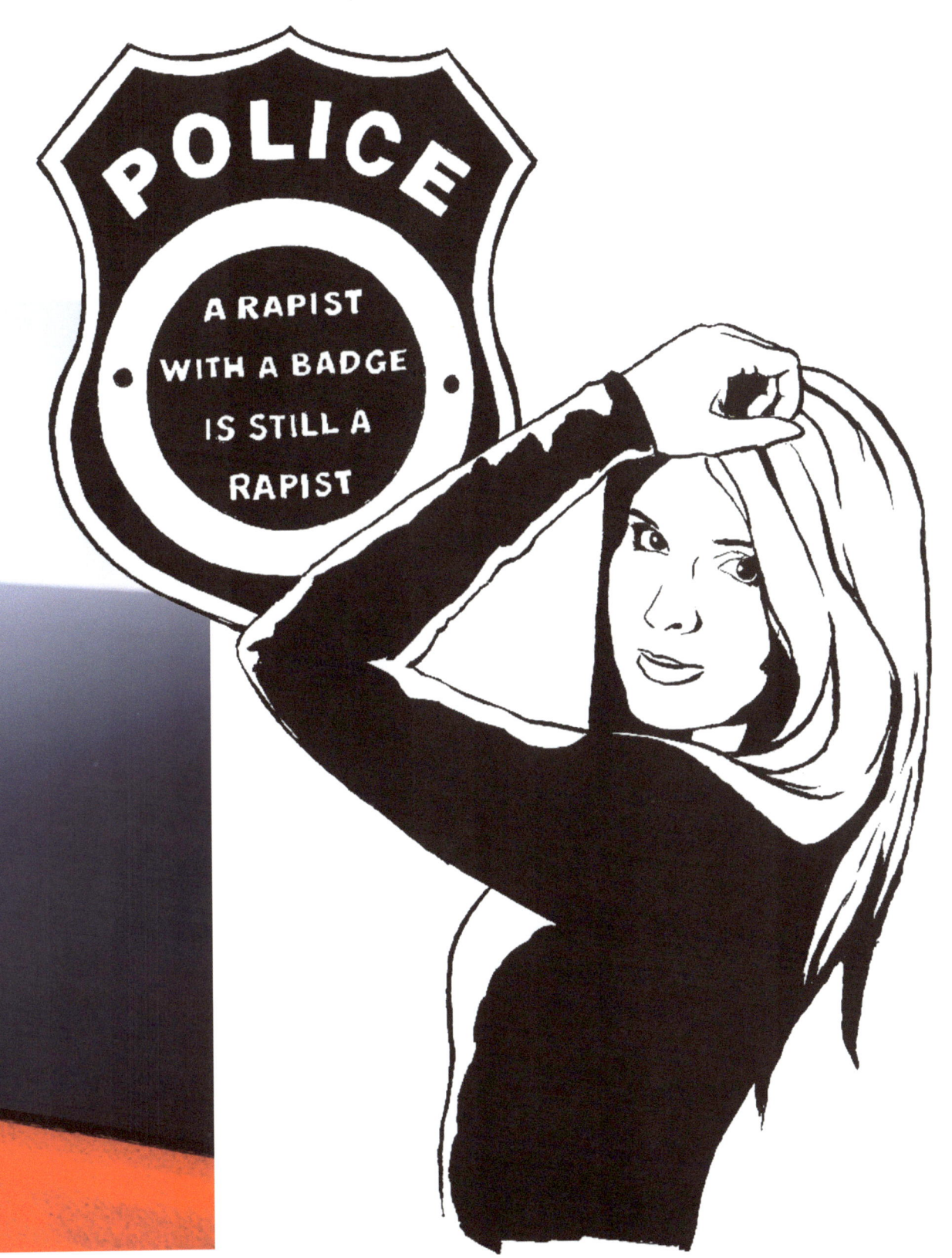

Drawing by Tiffany McCoy

joe-ann mathias

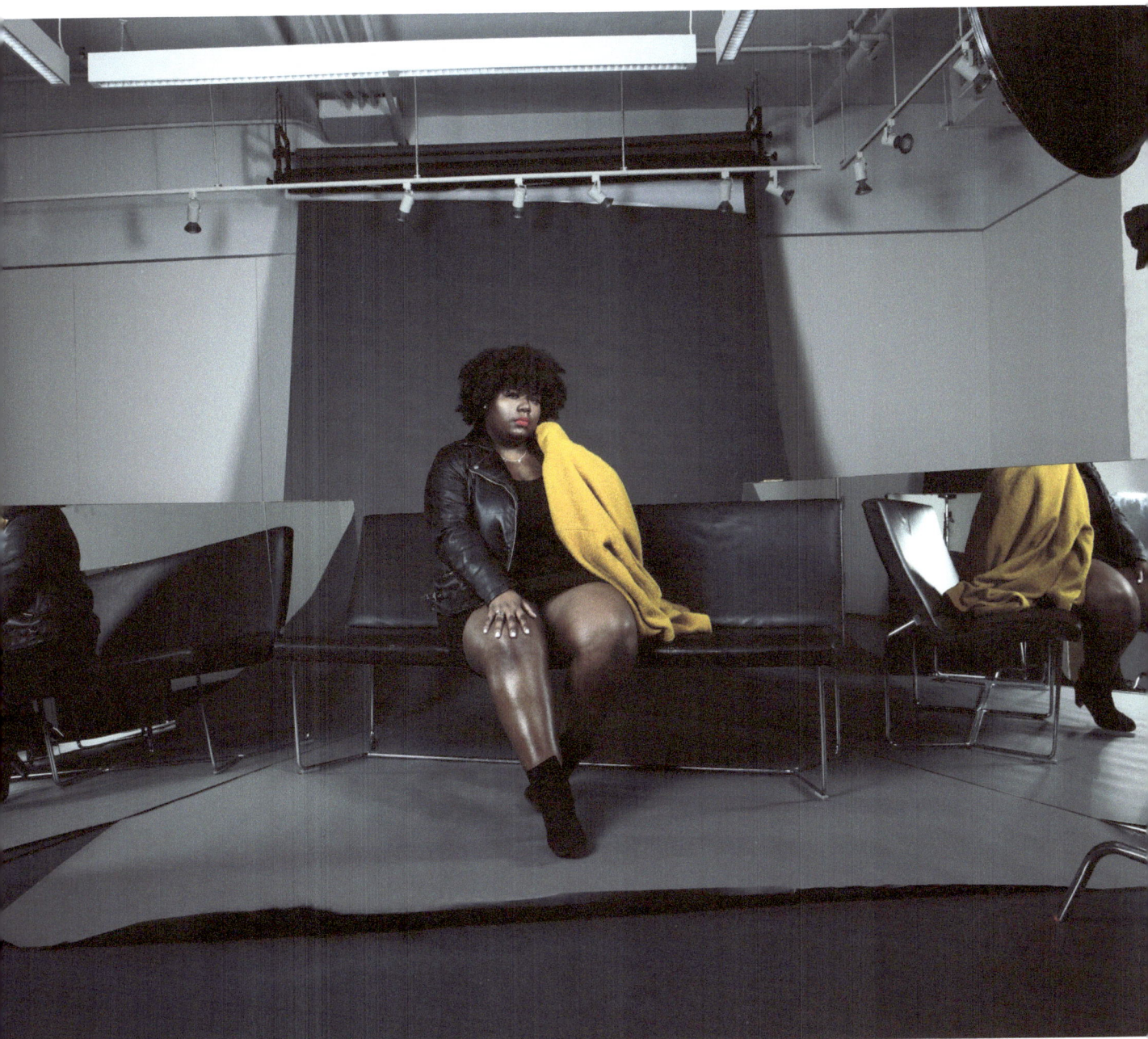

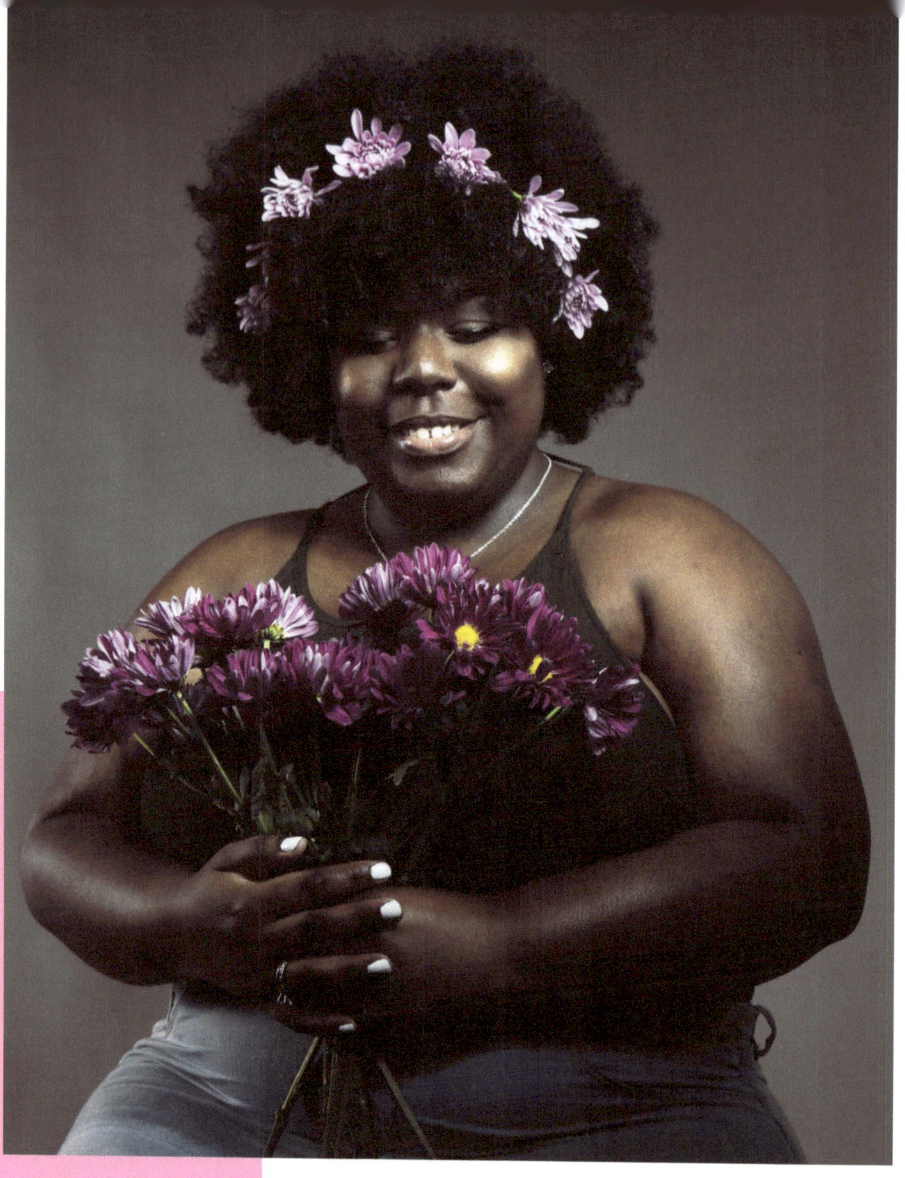

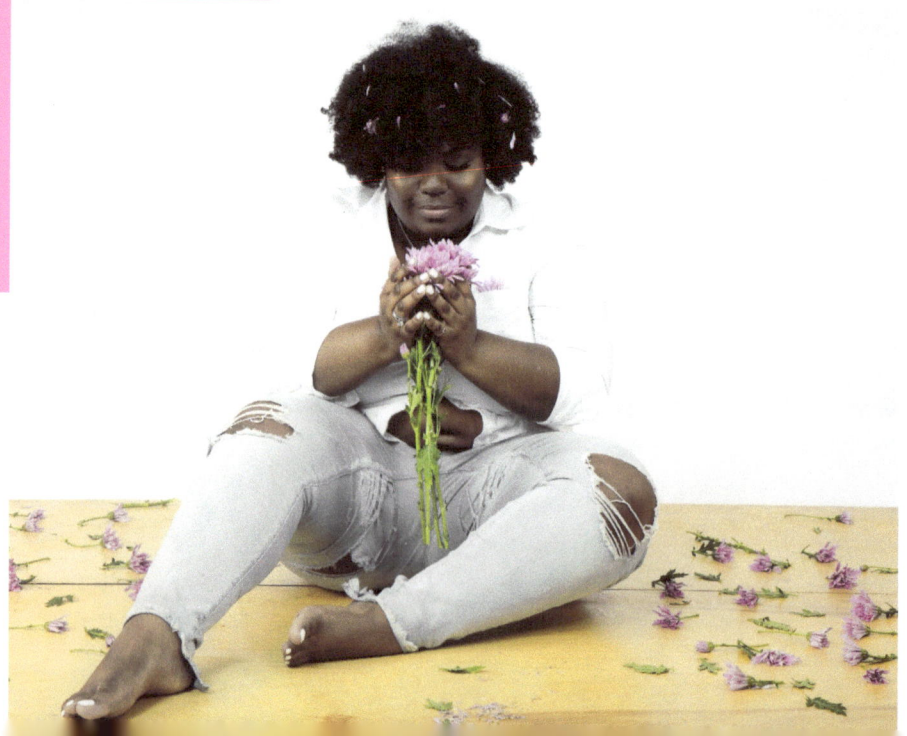

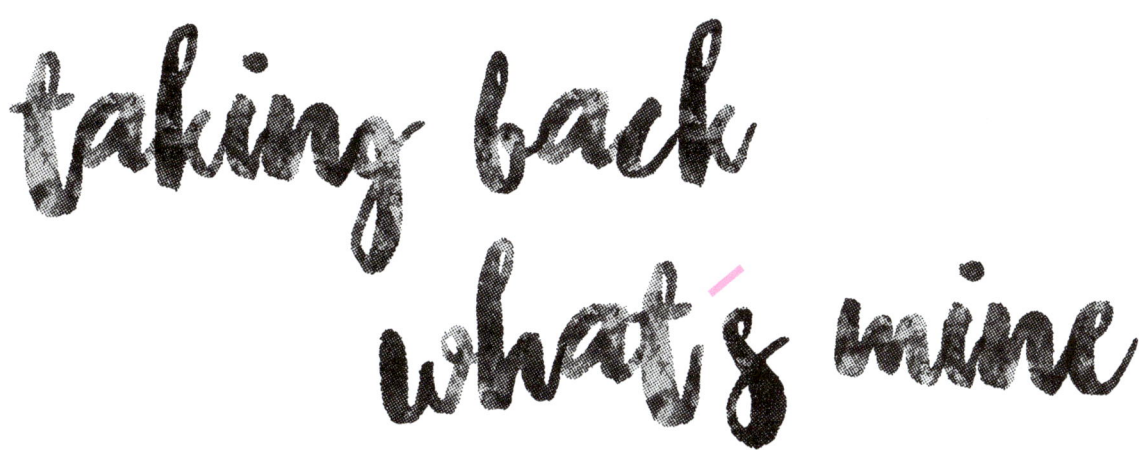

taking back what's mine

I am Perfect …. Just the way I am.
5'3, chocolate, with perfectly coiled black liquorice growing out of my scalp.
22 years young with a hell of a story to tell!
I am flawed ever so beautifully...
See I will not allow my hardships to own me …. I move with forgiveness ever so gracefully.
Everything I've ever went through … the good, the bad , and the ugly has all shaped me into the Queen that I was meant to be .
Don't you see …. The way my smile brightens up the room , body shape like a pear with a strong stance cause Baby I ain't goin nowhere , my hips sway as I walk away... I am the phenomenal woman maya was talkin bout! He thought passing me up was him taking a better route. But in all reality he was the one missing out. Cause if you thought you knew me then allow me to reintroduce myself. My name is JOE…. J to the O. E. I am a proud black woman who's finally free! Taking over the world you can call me Queen B
Don't bother wasting your time wondering how it came to be ….Just know that I found the secret to that self - love recipe! You can tell in the way I walk & the way I talk yall better get ready cause I'm reclaiming
This body and I'm reclaiming this heart !

CLAYTON BROWN

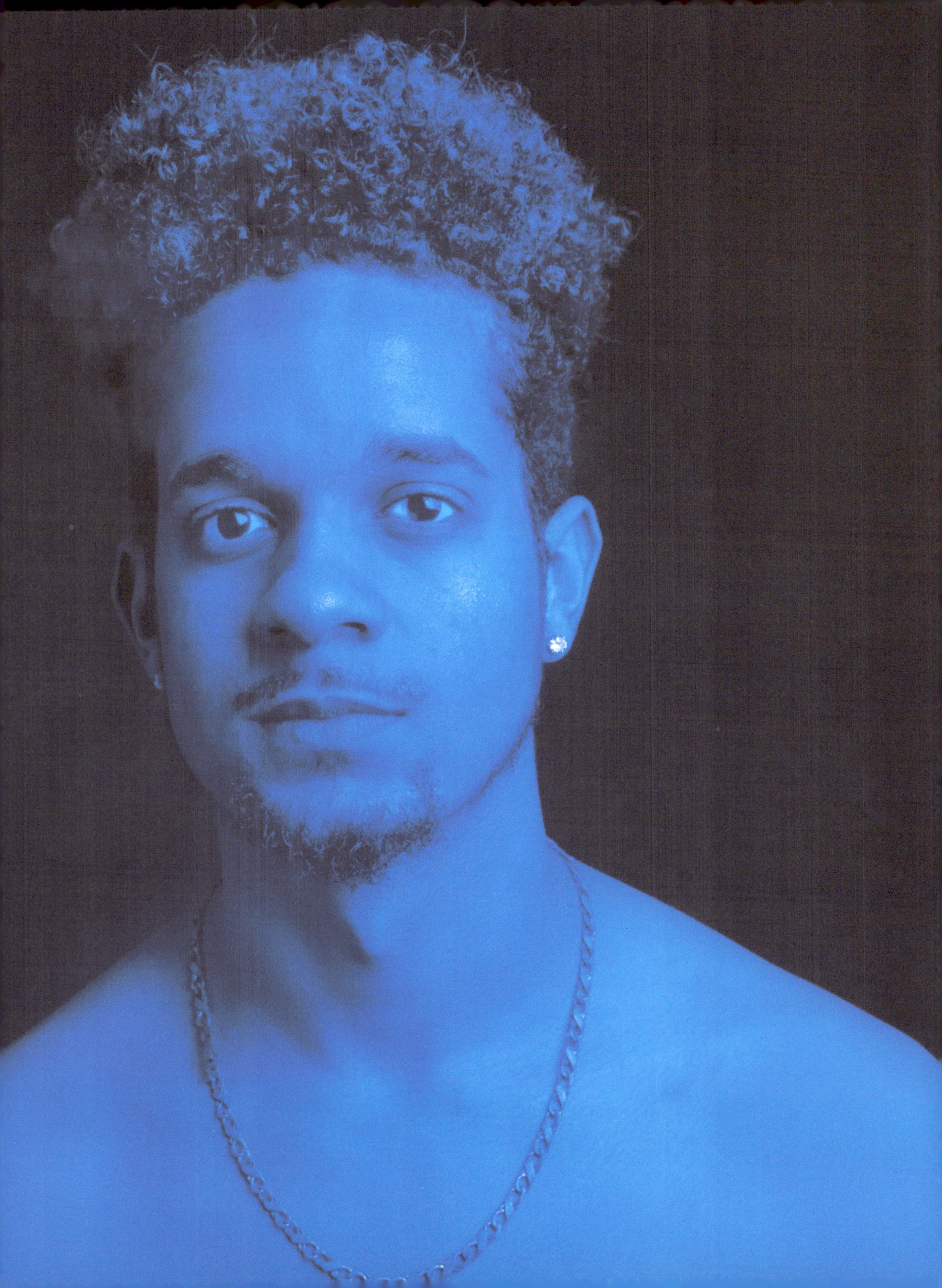

I WANTED TO USE THIS PHOTOSHOOT TO

showcase the different parts of myself. Some photos I look powerful and others I'm showing off my vulnerability. I really want others to know self expression is important, and so is self-love.

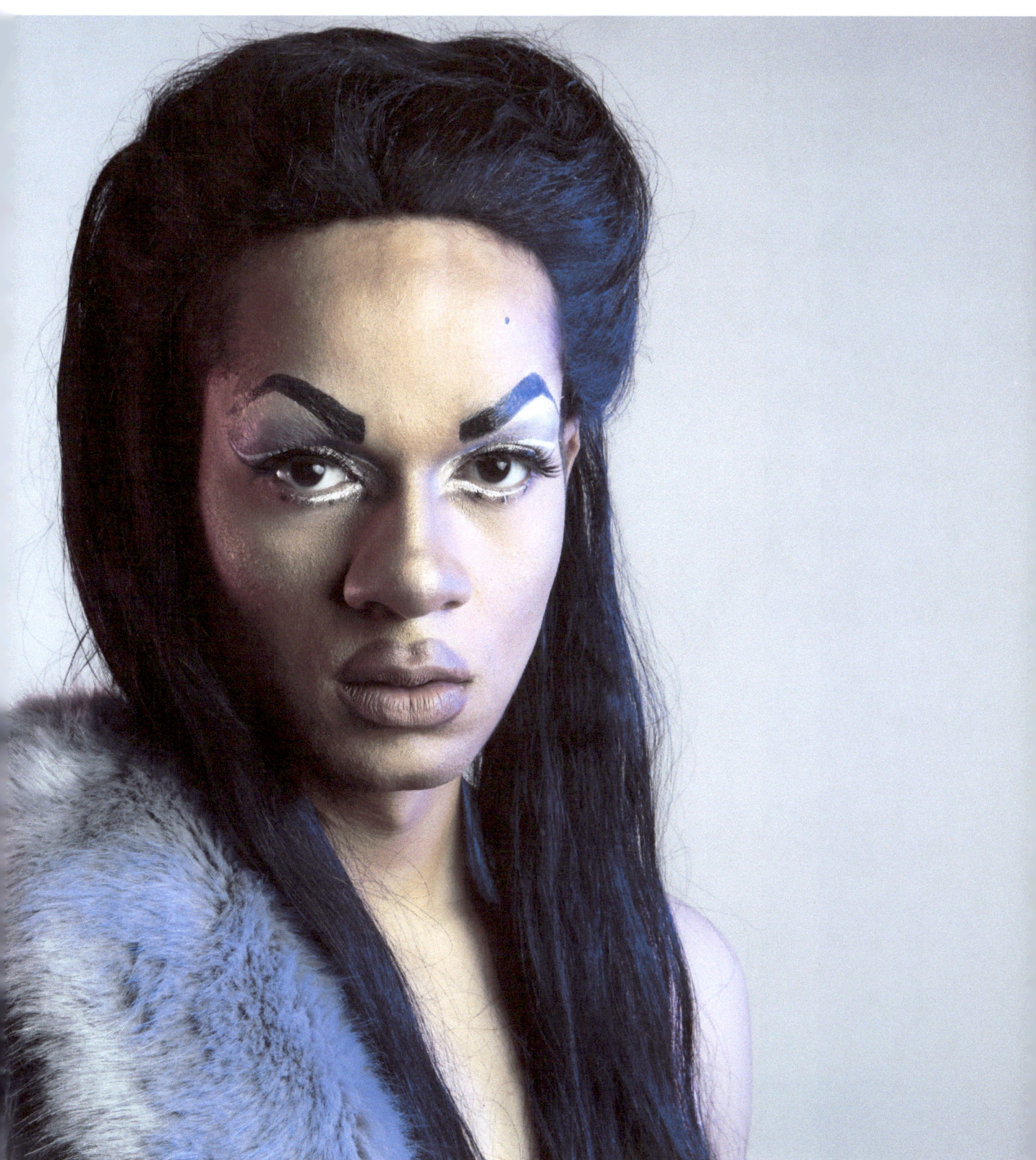

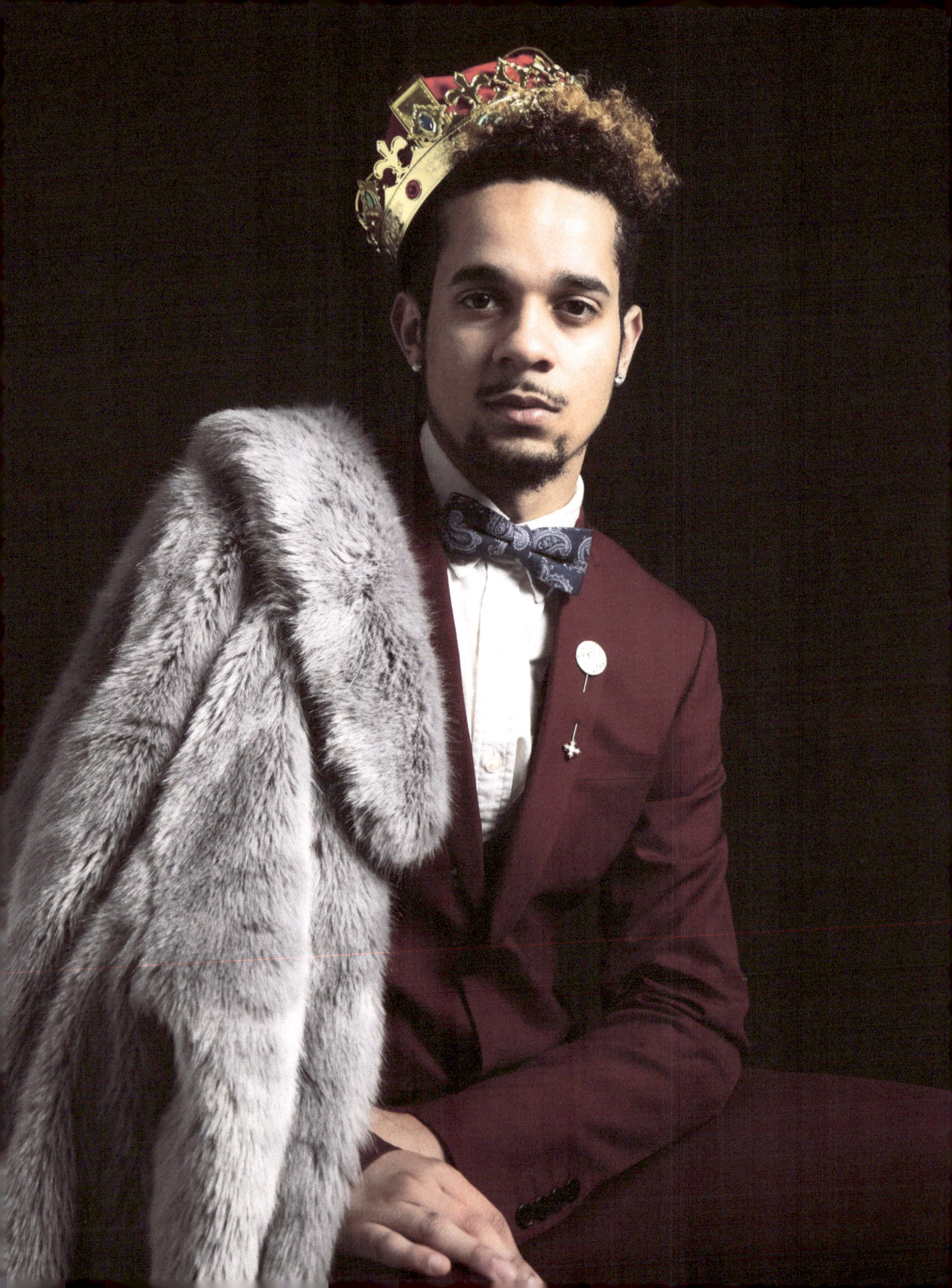

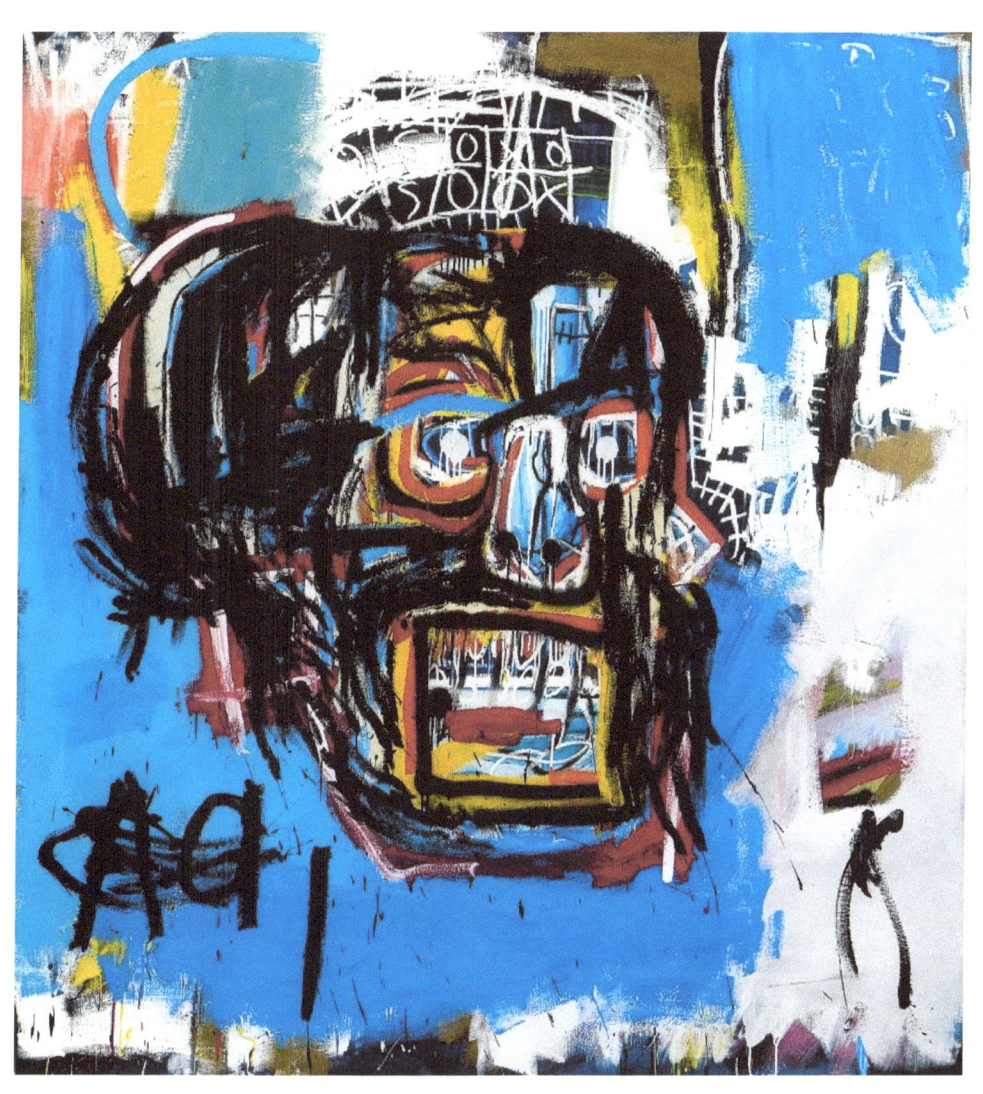

UNTITLED, 1982
JEAN-MICHEL BASQUIAT

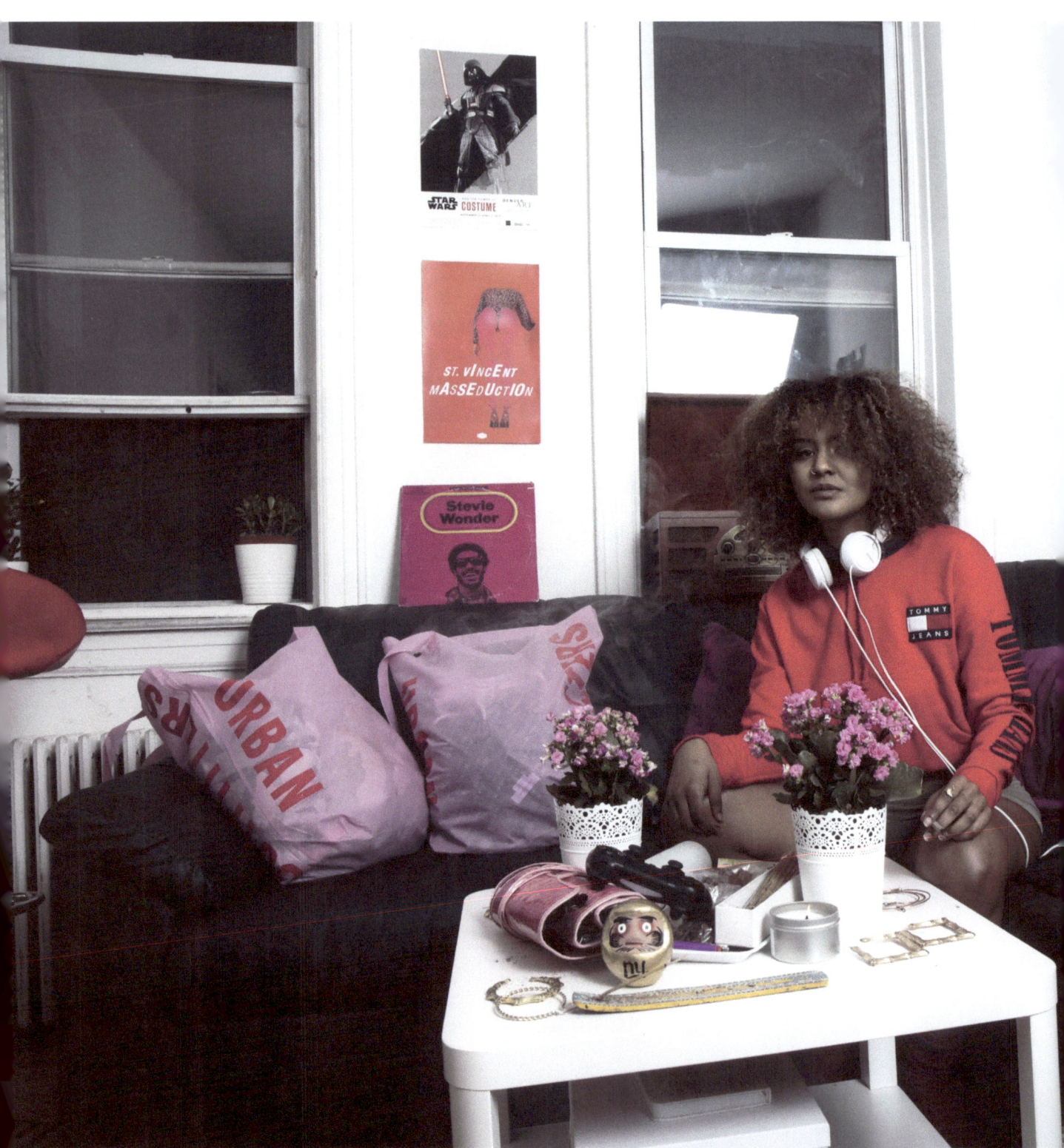

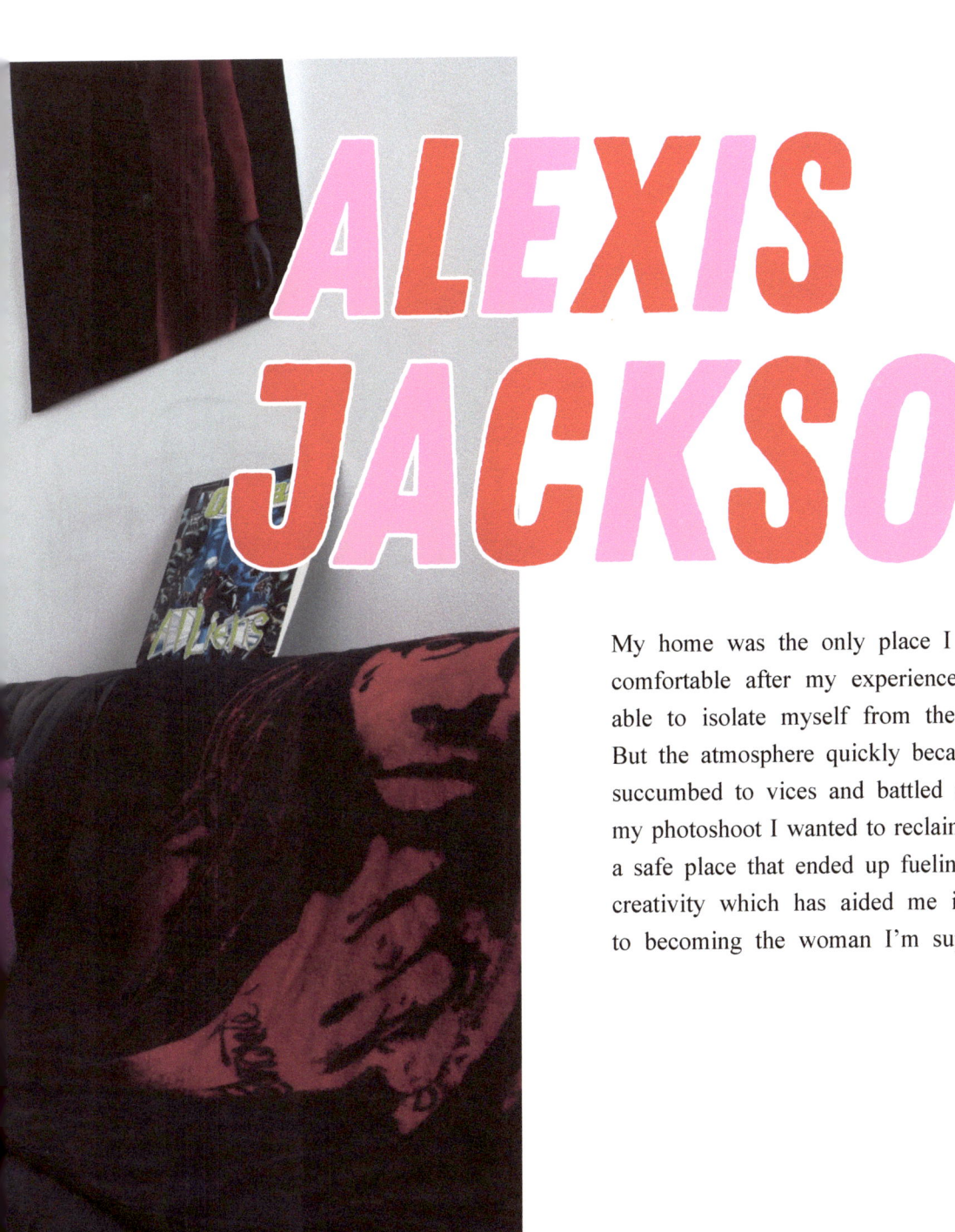

ALEXIS JACKSON

My home was the only place I felt safe and comfortable after my experience since I was able to isolate myself from the outer world. But the atmosphere quickly became toxic as I succumbed to vices and battled depression. In my photoshoot I wanted to reclaim my home as a safe place that ended up fueling my musical creativity which has aided me in my growth to becoming the woman I'm supposed to be.

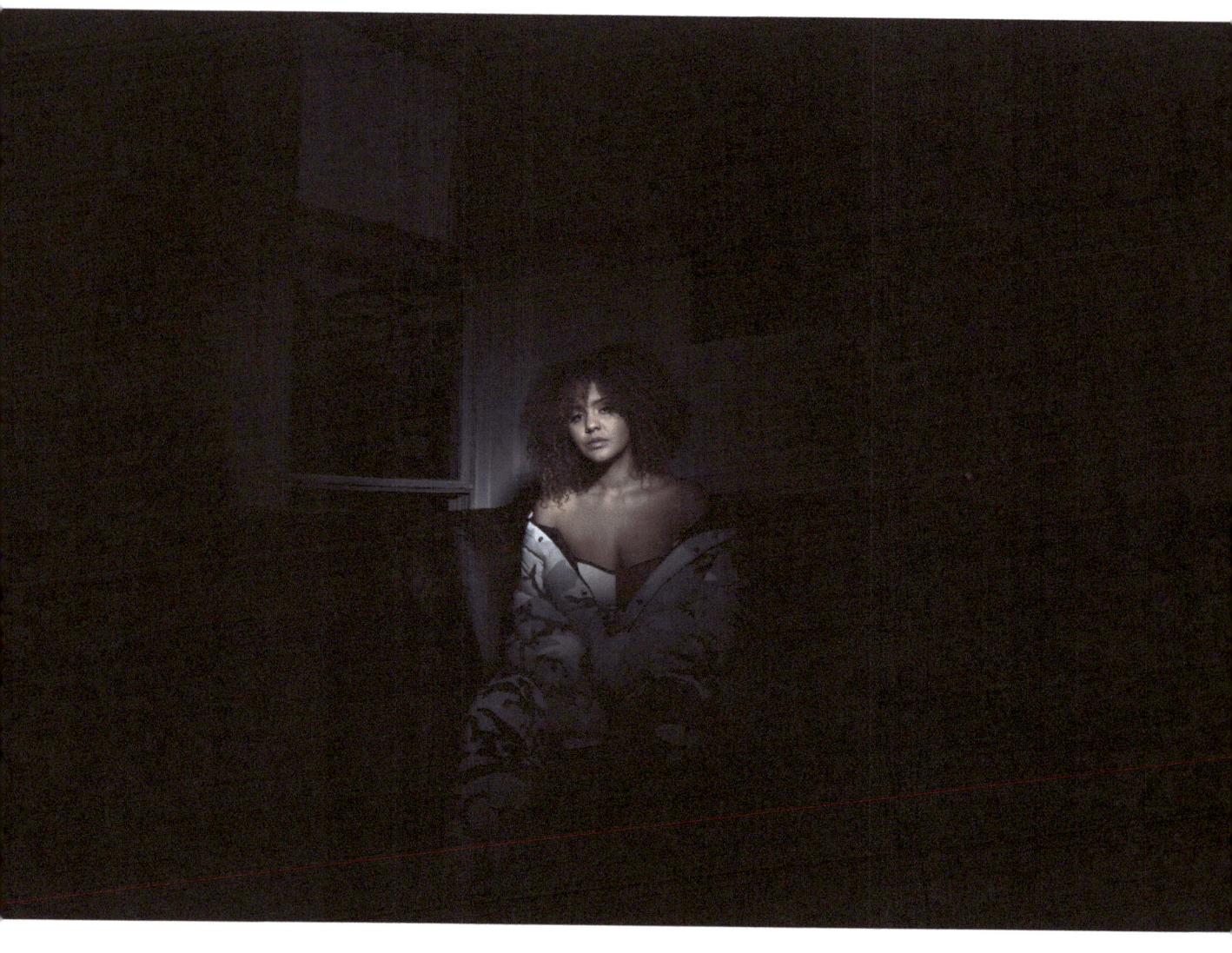

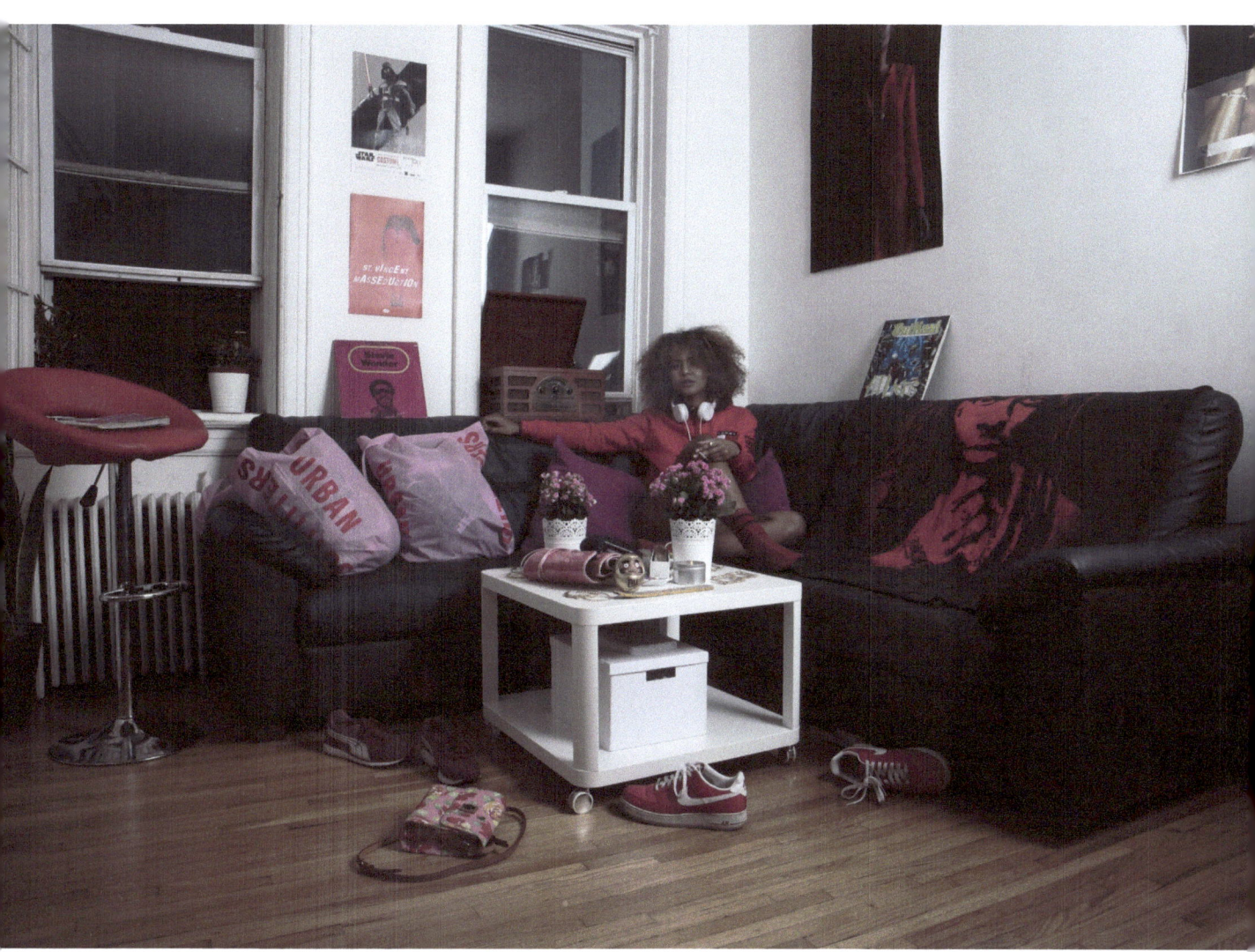

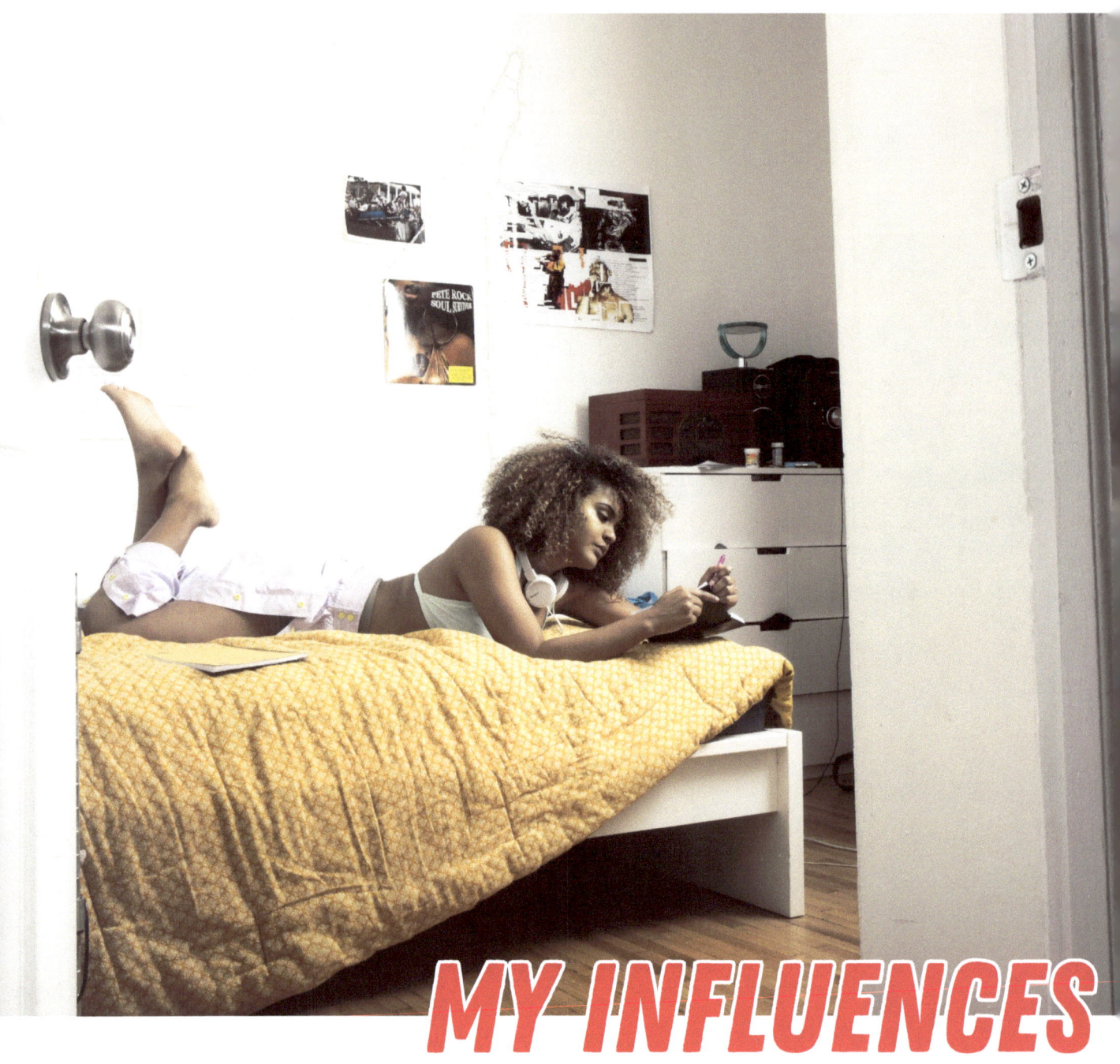

MY INFLUENCES
regarding both my music and social consciousness

- OUTCAST
- NAS
- TUPAC SHAKUR

LYRICS TO MY FAVORITE SONG:

I USED TO LOVE H.E.R.
BY COMMON

I might've failed to mention that this chick was creative
Once the man got to her, he altered her native
Told her if she got an image and a gimmick
That she could make money, and she did it like a dummy
Now I see her in commercials, she's universal
She used to only swing it with the inner-city circle
Now she be in the burbs, lookin' rock and dressin' hippie
And on some dumb shit when she comes to the city
Talkin' bout poppin' Glocks, servin' rocks and hittin' switches
Now she's a gangsta rollin' with gangsta bitches
Always smokin' blunts and gettin' drunk
Tellin' me sad stories, now she only fucks with the funk
Stressin' how hardcore and real she is
She was really the realest, before she got into showbiz
I did her, not just to say that I did it
But I'm committed (girl, he's committed) but so many niggas hit it
That she's just not the same lettin' all these groupies do her
I see niggas slammin' her, and takin' her to the sewer
But I'ma take her back, hopin' that the shit stop
'Cause who I'm talkin' about, y'all, is hip-hop

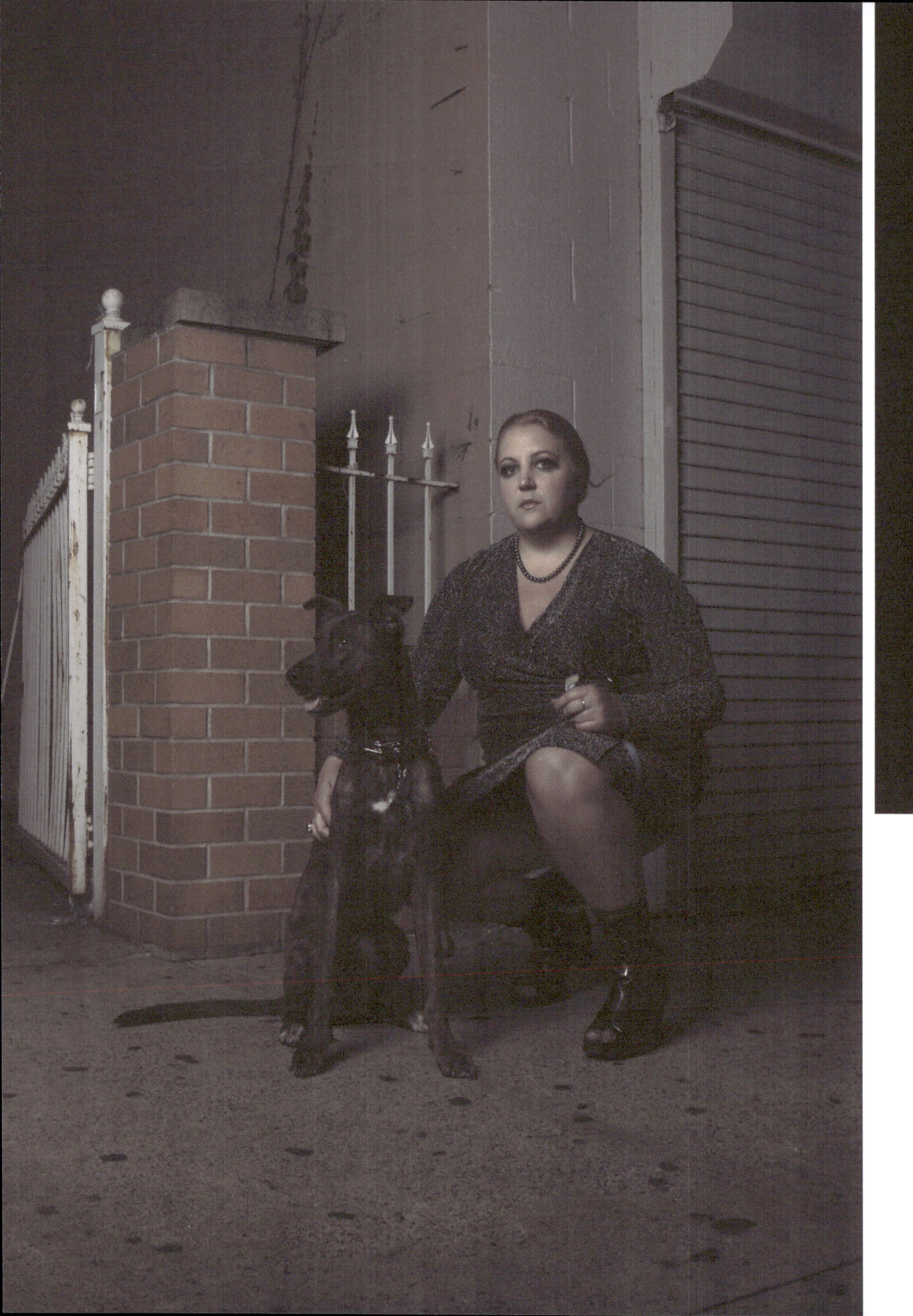

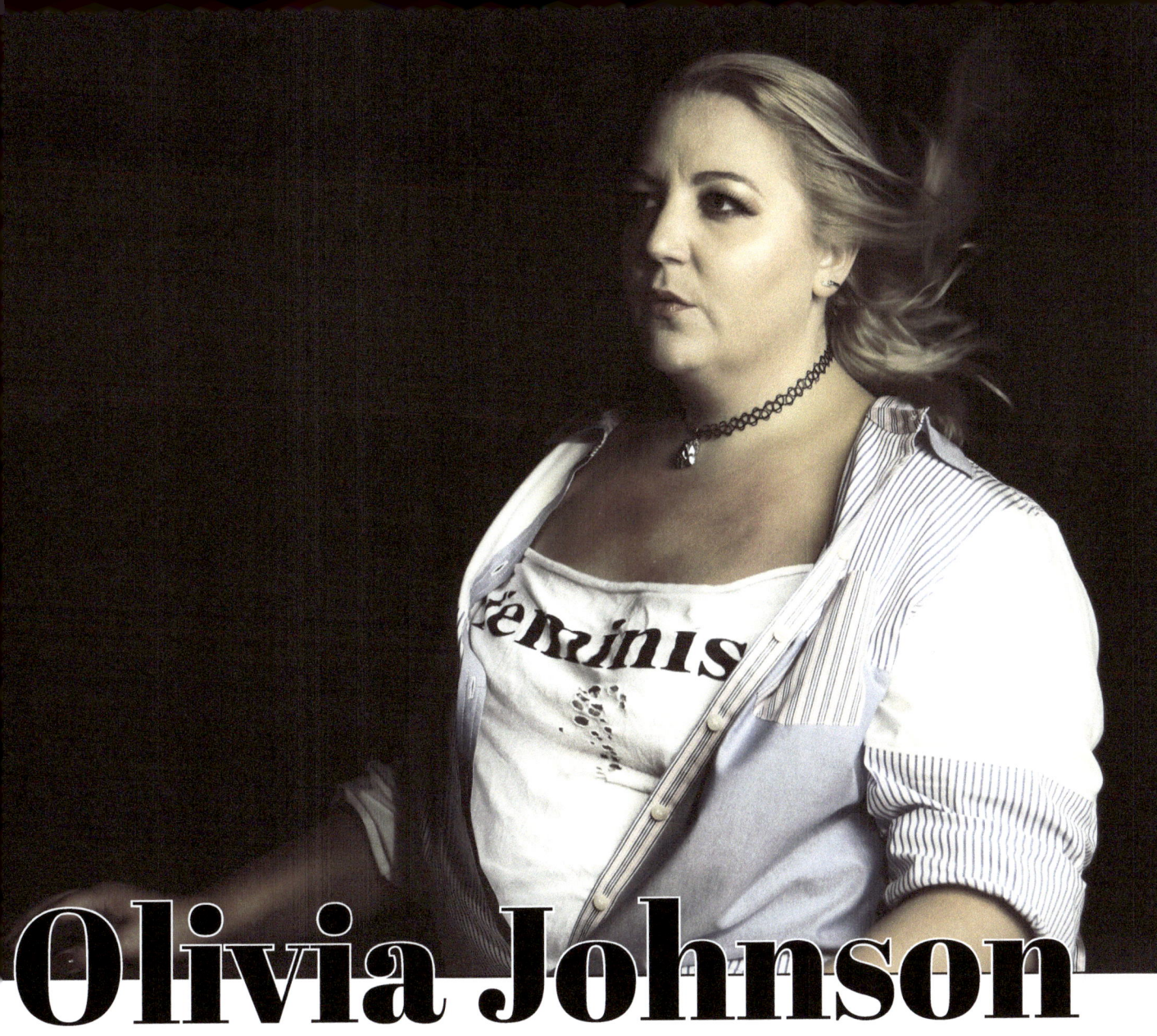

Olivia Johnson

This process with Survivors Magazine has been so cathartic. The photographs are a brave declaration that I will not be silent.

I'm very grateful for the opportunity to share my experiences and it was a privilege to do so with such a talented and articulate team.

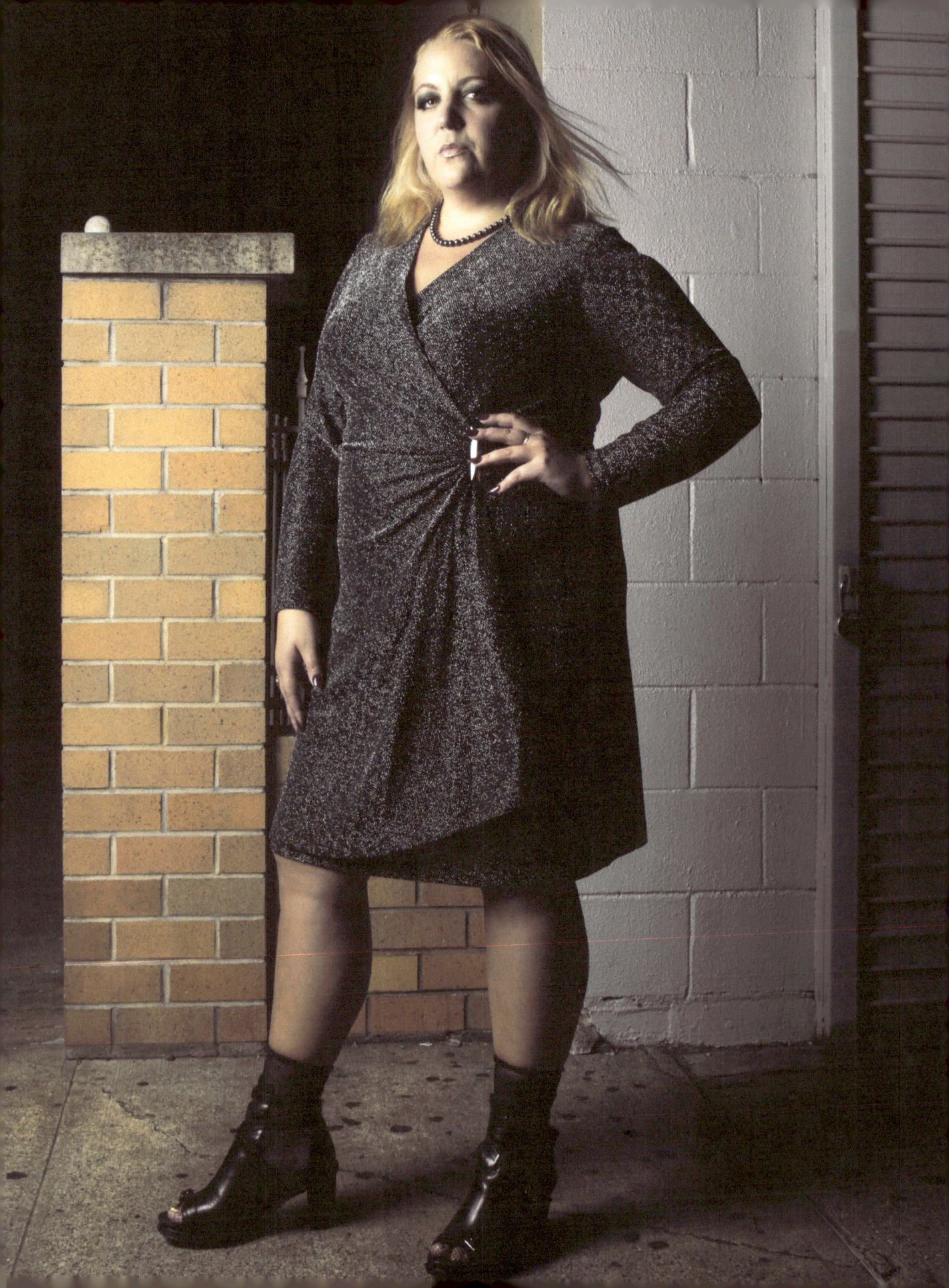

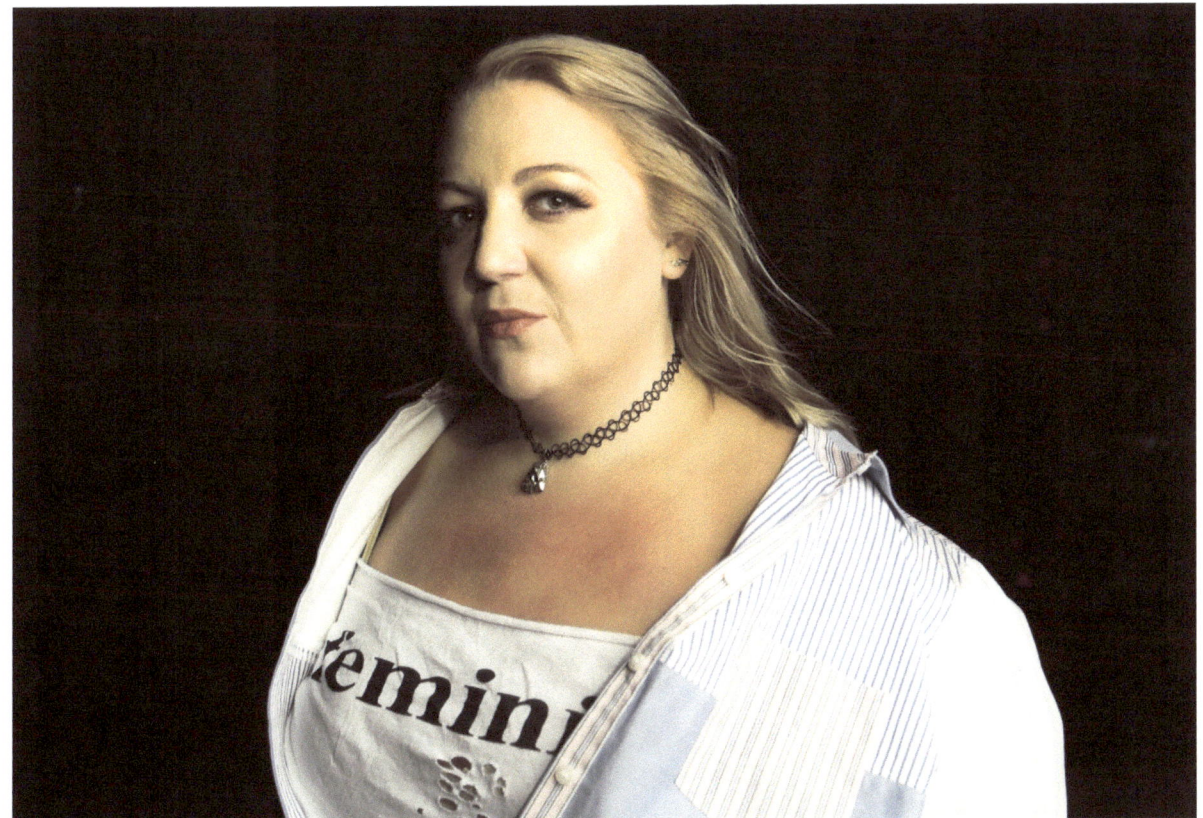

The first thing I did after I locked the door of my Bushwick apartment, was open the app and send off 103 characters to the Twitter timeline at 4am: So I was just followed from the train station and almost assaulted. As soon as he put his hands on me, I hit him and cussed him out

Under no circumstances did I want to call the police. I had yet to recognize what happened to me as a crime; I had dodged a scumbag who wanted to rape me, I got away, I wasn't the victim of a crime, I almost was. Plus I did not trust the cops and they were not going to protect me now. Instead, I chose to immediately put my words on the Internet, to confide in the semi-miscellaneous world wide web from my Twitter handle and to just let someone know something happened.

At the end of the week I reported the crime IRL to the 83rd precinct, was swept off to the Brooklyn SVU and participated in the exhausting, oppressive, biased, inefficient and archaic systems of law enforcement and criminal justice. Despite an investigation, no one was ever arrested; the rookie detective assigned to my misdemeanor sex crime, moved on to the next series of sex crimes, etc. My only take-away from that experience was the confirmation of the systems' deep futility and open discrimination against women and people of color by the NYPD.

What did prove true three years later, however, was the confidence I had in the Internet; I knew the power of putting my story out there, in my own words, for anyone to read. Years before #MeToo catalyzed a mainstream movement about being vocal about sexual assault and harassment, I was empowered by Feminista Jones' #YouOkSis and the @iHollaback campaign to be loud about street harassment online. This is and always has been a digital community where survivors are believed at all costs, experiences are validated, and as story after story is shared, this pandemic, pathological violence against women is exposed.

You cannot tell us it isn't real, for there is strength in numbers and healing in these hashtags.

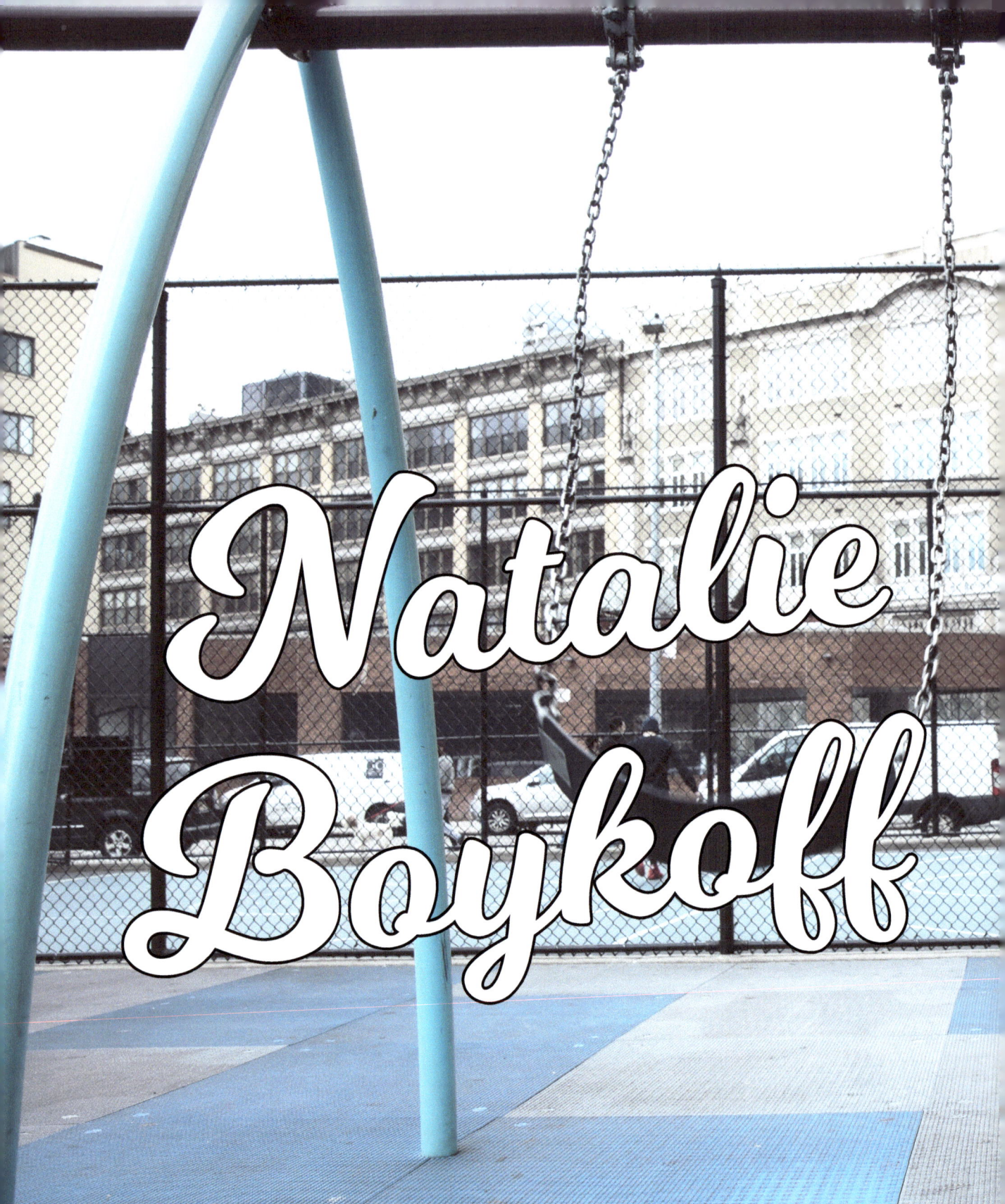

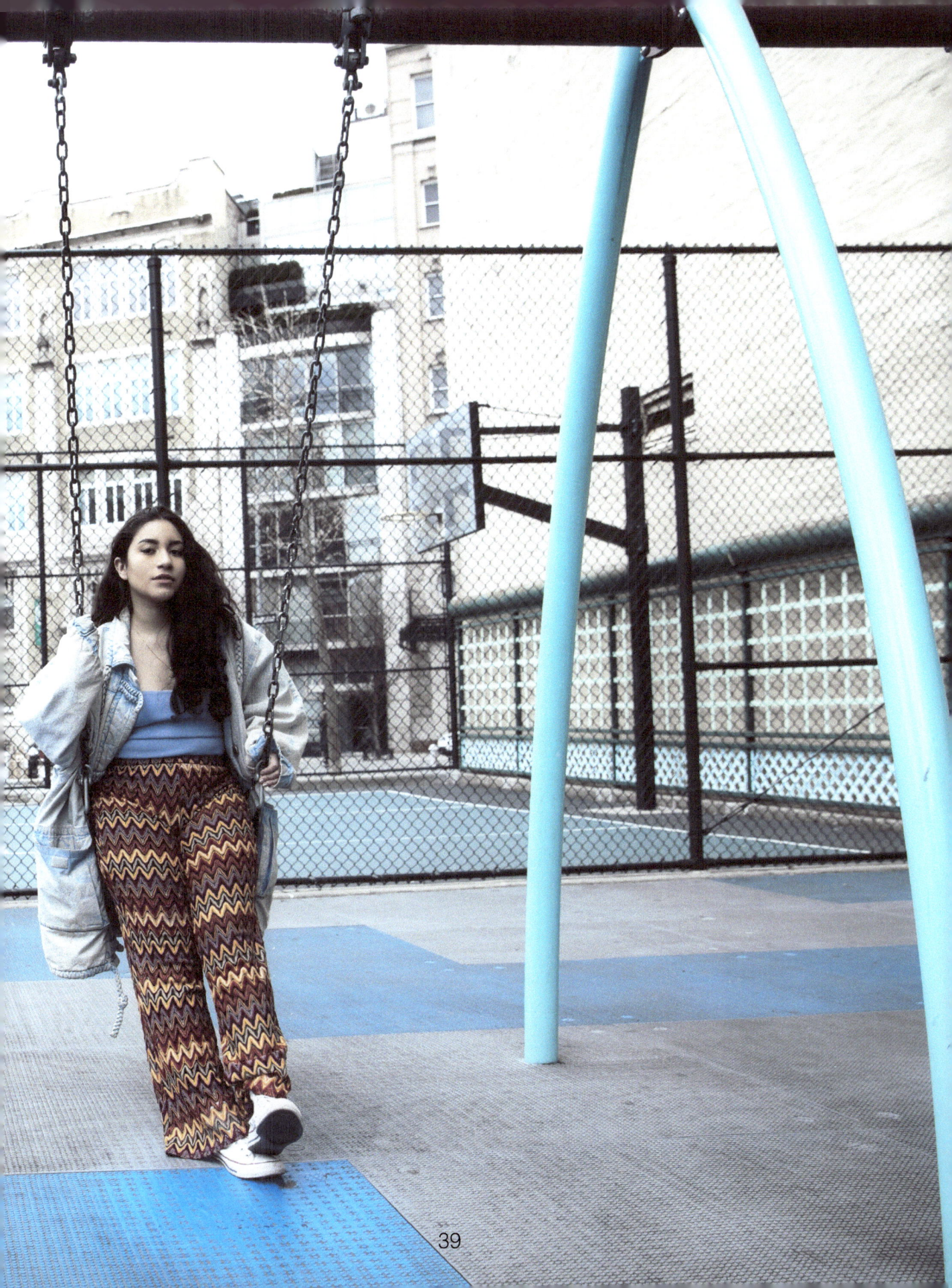

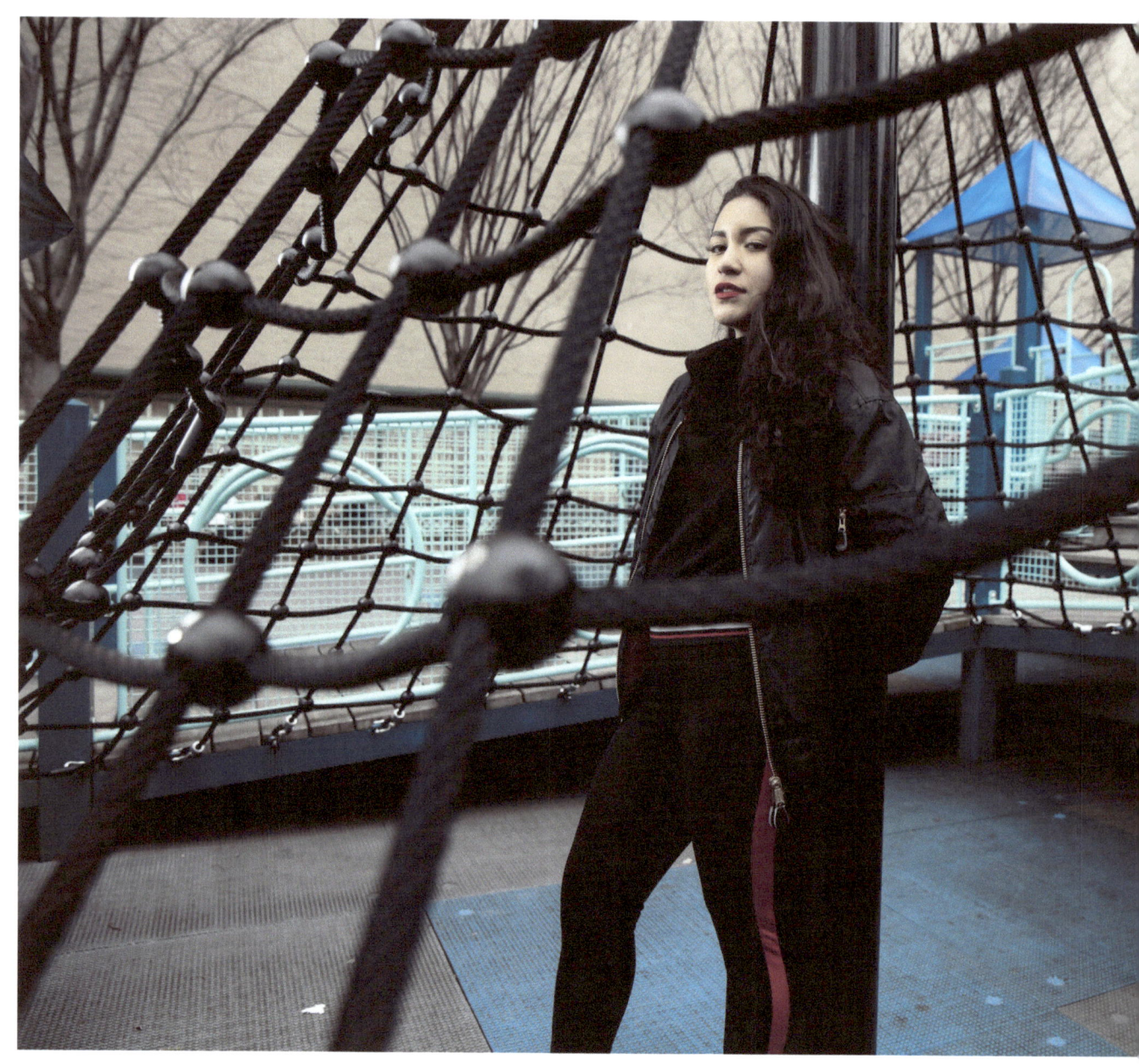

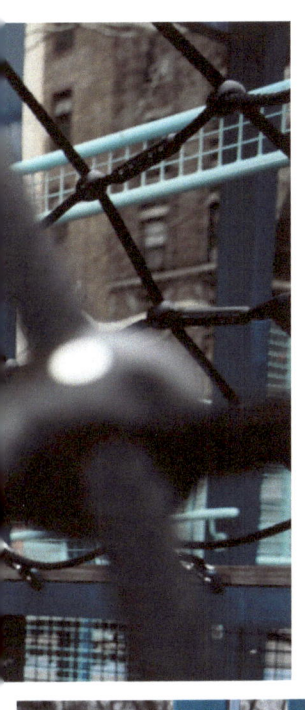

> I decided to hold my photo shoot in the playground where I spent my adolescent years because this period was crucial to corrupting the development of my own sexual autonomy. After experiencing sexual violence at the start of college, I further internalized that shame, causing delays in getting the resources I needed to start recovery. This photo shoot is about the process of relieving myself from that shame and reclaiming agency that is meant to highlight the resiliency I've found in myself throughout college.

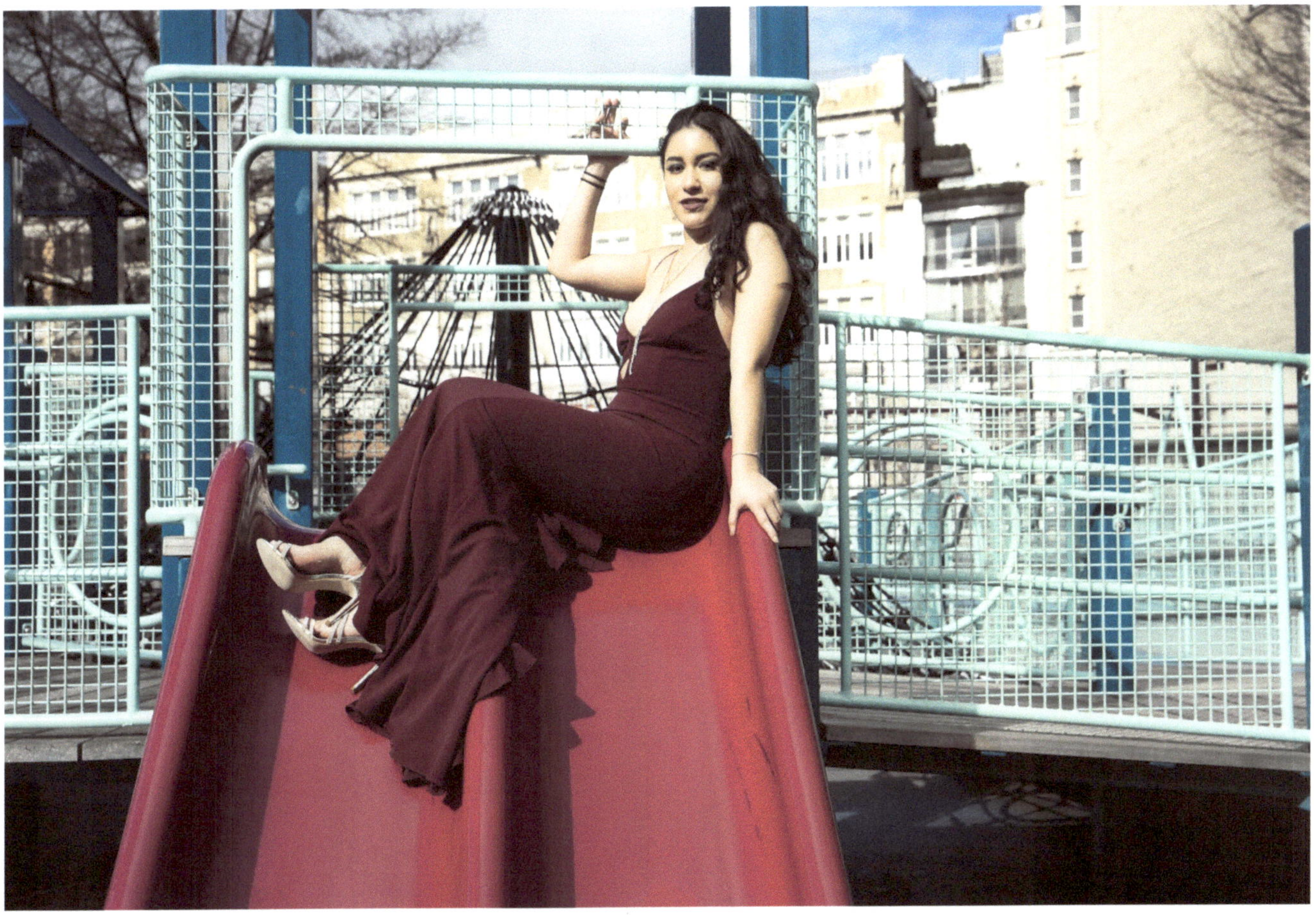

Ocean Of Shame

When I was 13 years old, I thought I had power in being objectified.
I let these boys teach me what to do with my body,
and with every touch I became more useful, more desired,
but it was never enough.
I became blind to my own choice, my own freedom,
and then I got caught between two polarizing currents,
one tugged me out to sea where my sole purpose was to please those who gazed upon me,
the other pulled me under where my very existence was to be shamed and drowned,
either way I lost sight of the shore.
Isolated,
I had to comfort myself in the absence of land
where I couldn't stand,
and this delusion of power,
I clung to it as though it was a life raft.

When I was 18 years old, I lost all power.
Two months into college, my fresh start,
I was dragged so far down into that ocean,
I forgot in which direction the surface was.
Hitting rock bottom,
alone,
I was preparing to live in this darkness as it became my only surrounding,
assault, followed by abuse,
followed by another assault...
And that shame was the only thing able to grow in the darkness.
It said:
why were you drinking,
it's your fault,
how could you let this happen twice,
there must be something wrong with you.

When I was 20 years old, I got angry.
I didn't recognize myself in the burst of uncontrollable rage
and I liked that.
Finally, I had resurfaced,
I could breathe again.
I started to realize that
given the way I was made to feel like the violation of my body was okay,
the shame produced
from every bit of abuse
was inevitable.
In fact,
It was only fitting
that a boy who grew up with all of his friends objectifying me,
ended up raping me
because I was not the only one being taught that my body was there for the taking.

Today, I'm reclaiming my body
that only I was born with the power over,
with all its imperfections and complex desires,
with all it's pain and all it's resiliency.
I'm arriving at the shore,
I haven't felt in so long,
releasing that shame,
and replacing it with love.

Ramzi Shatara

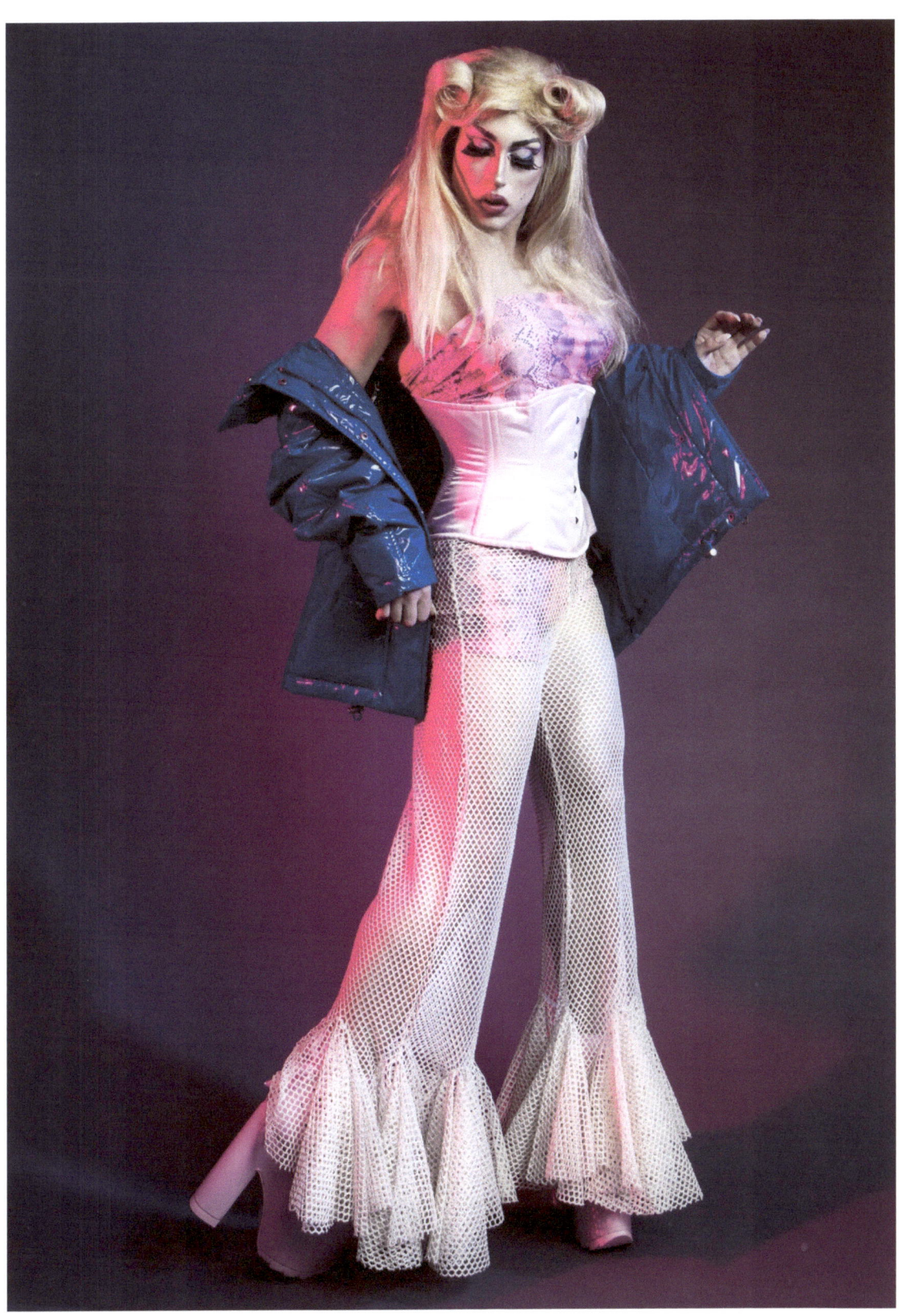

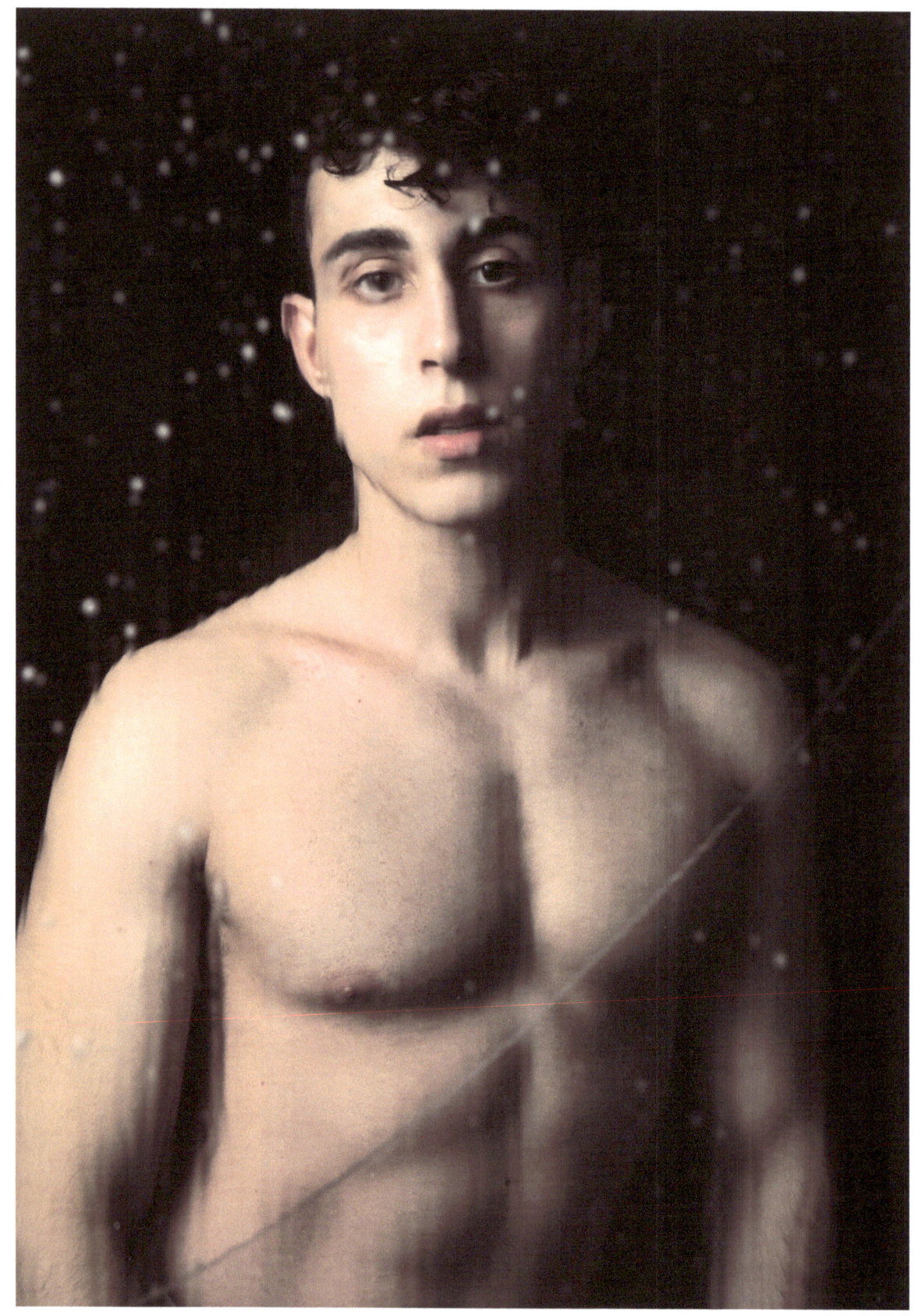

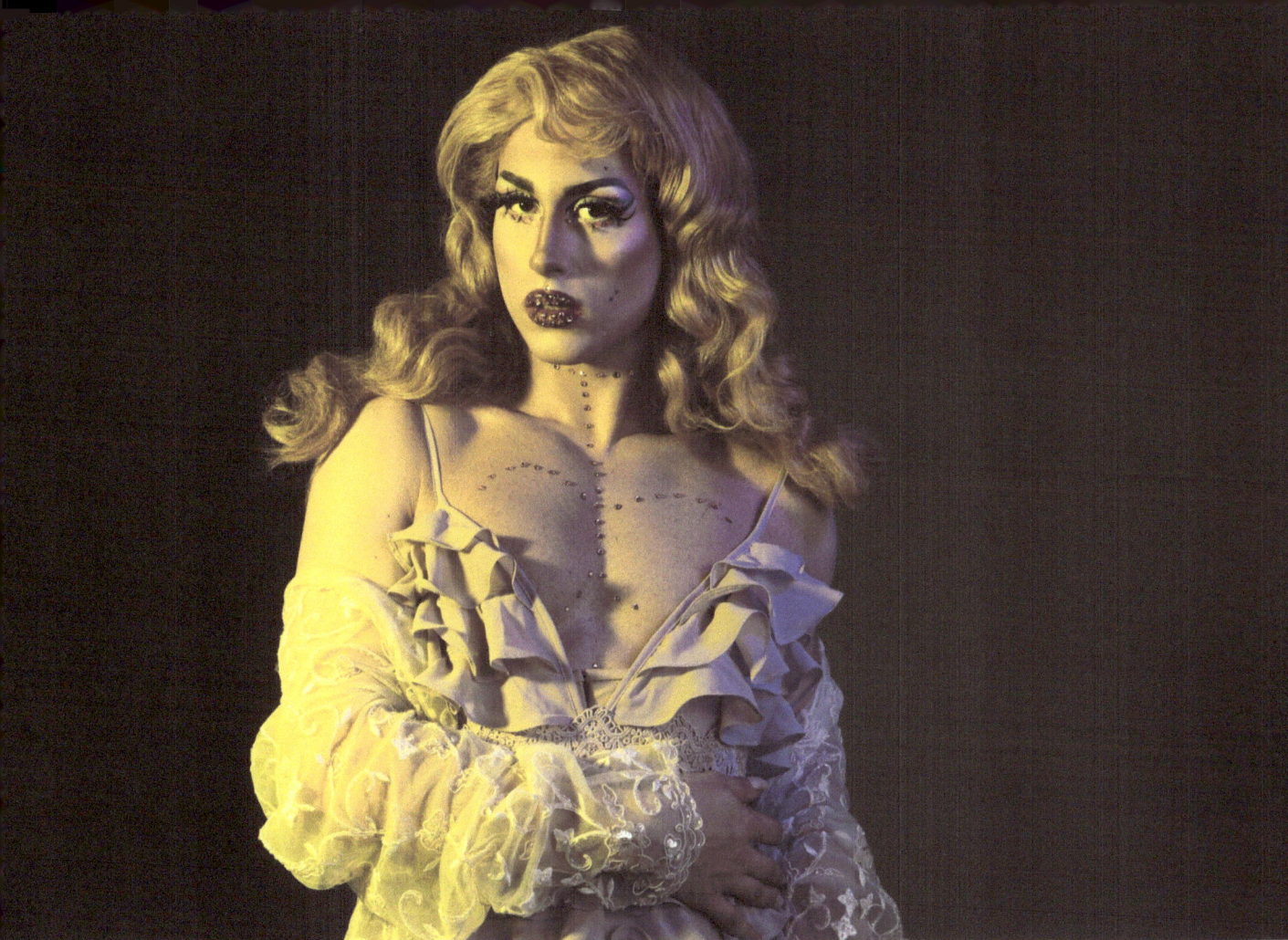

From Grand Ballroom: a Visual Album (2019)

I wish that the men who invaded my body were dead. I dream of their skulls being slowly pulled out of their skin by a single string and I wish their dicks would fall off by someone merely blowing air at them. I wish I didn't hate so fiercely because men like you taught me how to hate myself. I wish that every time I said the word rape people's eyes wouldn't bulge out of their heads as though I sinned. As though I should be ashamed of a crime I didn't commit. I wish a lot of things. I wish i could pull myself apart into a hill of limbs and organs that denote no sexual energy or tension, so that the fear of being desirable dissipates. It is a sad thing to fear—being desirable. Why am I still paying when I am bereft of any sexual currency? I still pray they find me beautiful because we have been calibrated to believe that is the only revenge. I find myself accepting a distortion of love and believing that it is love itself. I have swallowed only fragments of its sensation and those jagged shards sliced my insides into a stream of tissue that knows nothing but to cry. You tricked my body and now it tricks me into seeing torture as love.

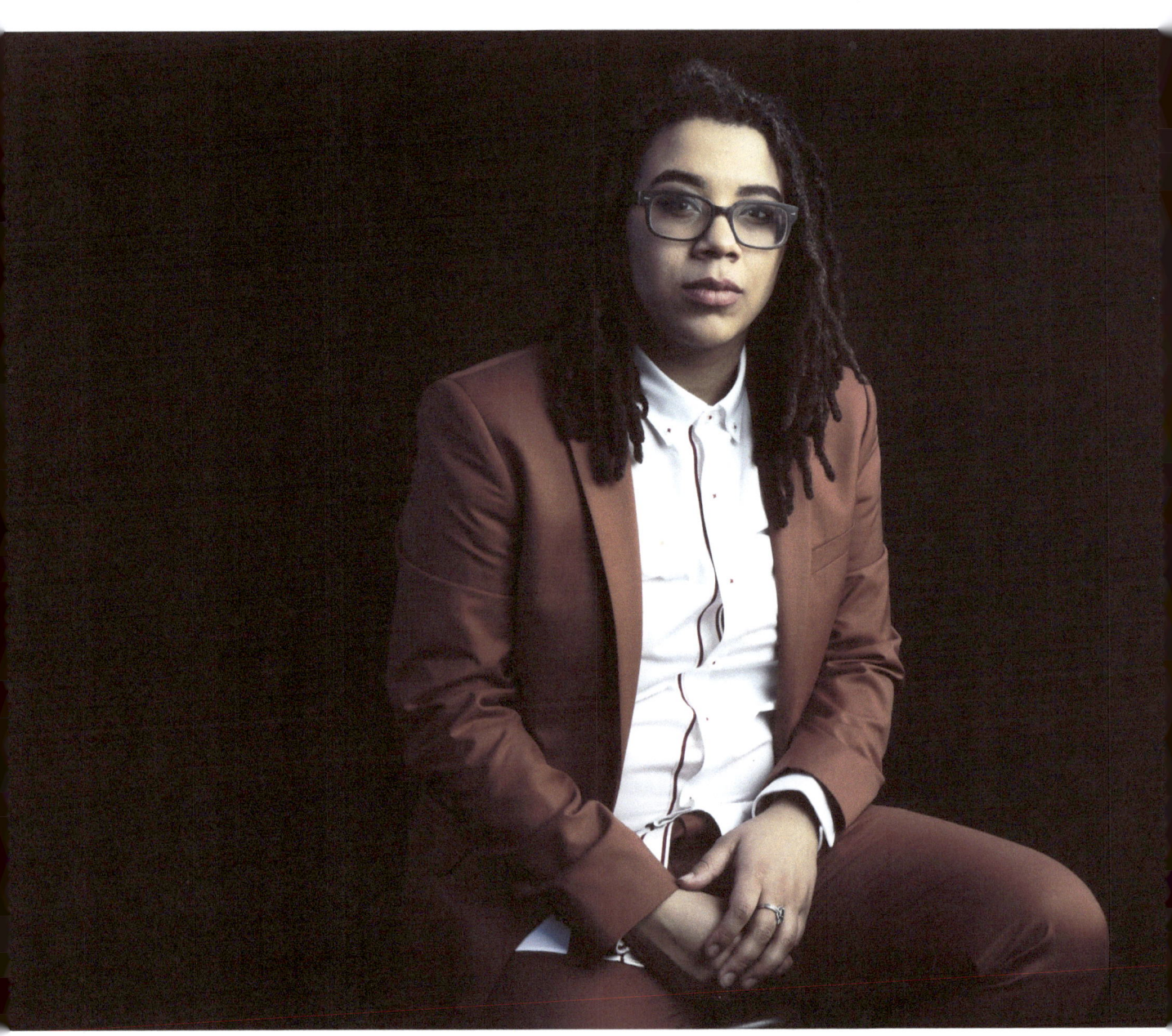

NELLY BESS

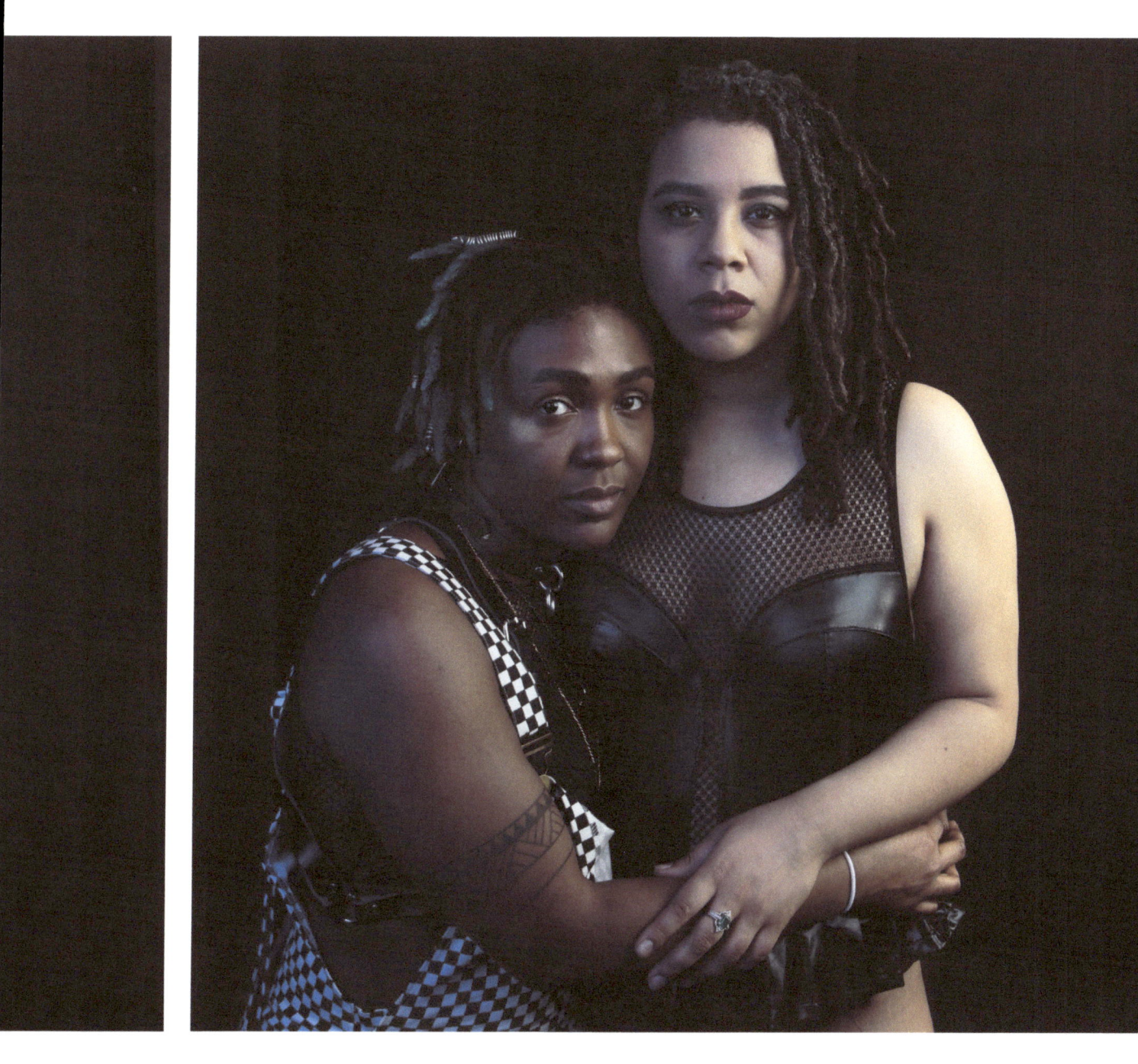

I did the photo shoot to prove this body deserves to take up space, more than just the space in a therapist office, or the space between healing and learning how to breathe again. Reading up on sexual trauma I never find stories from people who look like me, and I wanted to change that. In this shoot, I wanted to show how finding a partner who didn't let my trauma make them want me any less, helped me find healing through Kink.

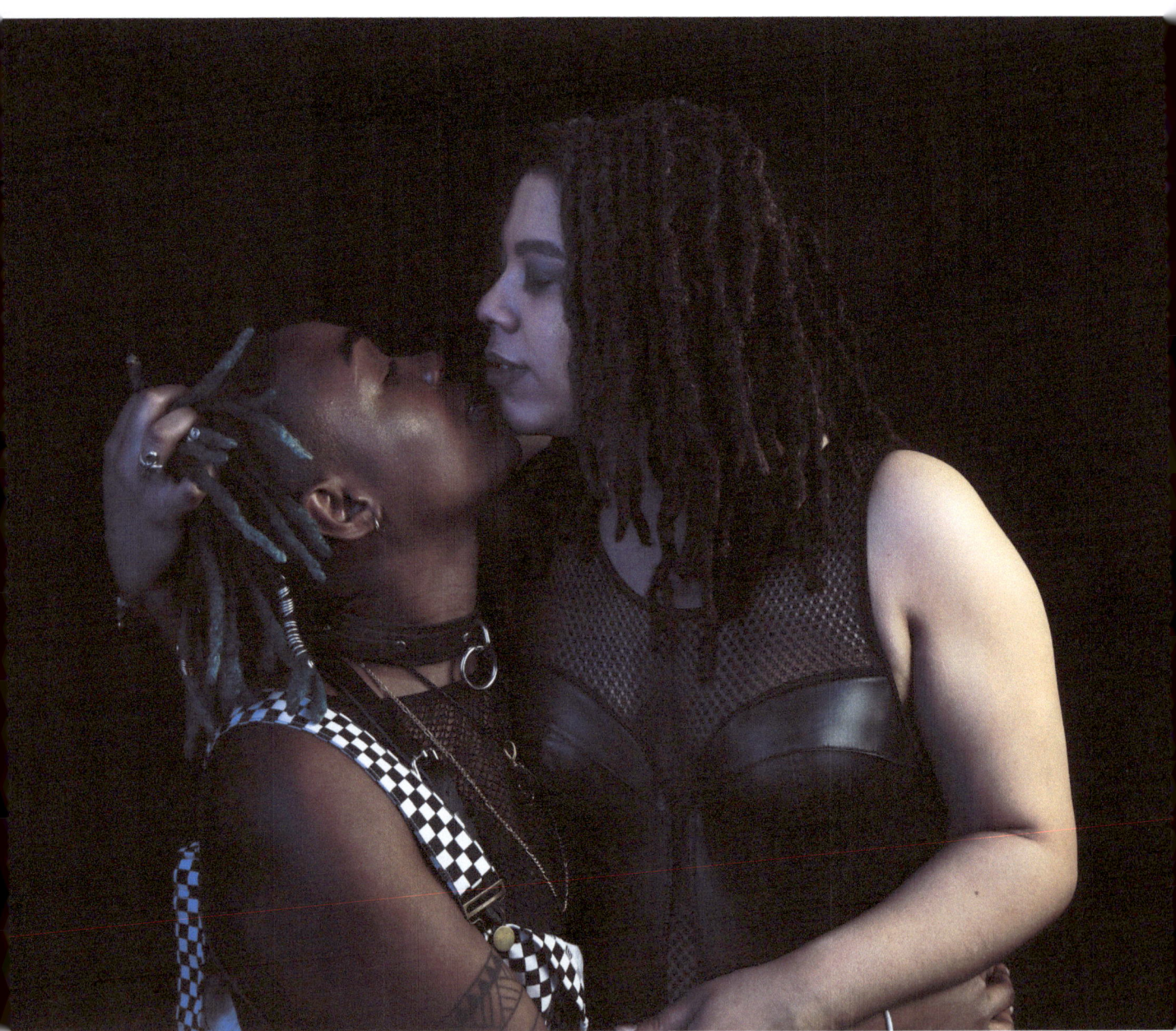

NO RESPONSE

When my friend stumbles
Across a pregnancy test on the car ride home
She will not ask if it is mine

She will assume it was for someone else
Like the Pharmacist
Apologizing for accidentally calling me "Sir"

It's funny how people will dismiss possibility
On appearance alone

When dikes cry rape
That is eyewitness enough

Masculinity the perfect alibi
To prove he wasn't where my rapekit
Said he was

The world says they can't believe why a straight man
would want to touch someone that looked like a boy

Like choice of clothing has ever been permission for the grieving

As if sexual assault
Only likes a particular kind of woman
And I can't be its type

My rapist said I was too pretty to be gay

so the thought of morning sickness
Left no room to proces

I question
When I cum
Whether it was something I willingly gave
Or something stolen

When I can't for my girlfriend
I wonder if my body
Knows how to give
If it isn't being forced first

When my body goes quiet
Because it still hasn't forgiven me
For letting this happen

Cannot bring itself to make a sound
Like my mother's mouth
When she first found out

The first time my hands belong to me again
I touched her like hindsight
Tried to remember what my own body sounded like

Wondered
If she cums
Whose fault was it?

Is it hers if her body responds?

I know response has a mind of its own

The therapist says cumming during a sexual assault is common

I think about the last time
We both were competing to apologize for the flash back

Trauma a pile of receipts
She's has had to pay for when I have nothing left to give

Said the wrong name out during sex
wish it was someone I cheated with
something she could hate me for

Us becoming an open relationship with my sadness
My therapist reiterates
Healing is never a one time thing

I say
Victim and survivor
Is broken spelled the same way

what is healing but the world forcing you to believe
You are not allowed to be sad anymore

First time I came since the rape

She'll confuse my body trying to drown itself to death
As an orgasm

Mistake an open wound

As a vagina

Pry me open like the court case
we've both avoid mentioning
Swallow my guilt

Her mouth trying to suck the poison out
Suffocate the memory

both soaking in a trigger

My sweat a fever breaking
Reminding us that I am still unwell

Despite how healthy I looked
Damaged comes in multiple outfits
when you thought you've outgrown it
when it doesn't fit the same way

My tongue a conveyor belt of baggage
Of all the parts that have yet to call themselves survivors
begging to be fixed back into a person

How long does time need to heal so I can have my future back?
I've been a person
Before the assault
And after
But sex will make my body a reminder
Every time When I undress myself
People will always see the rape first

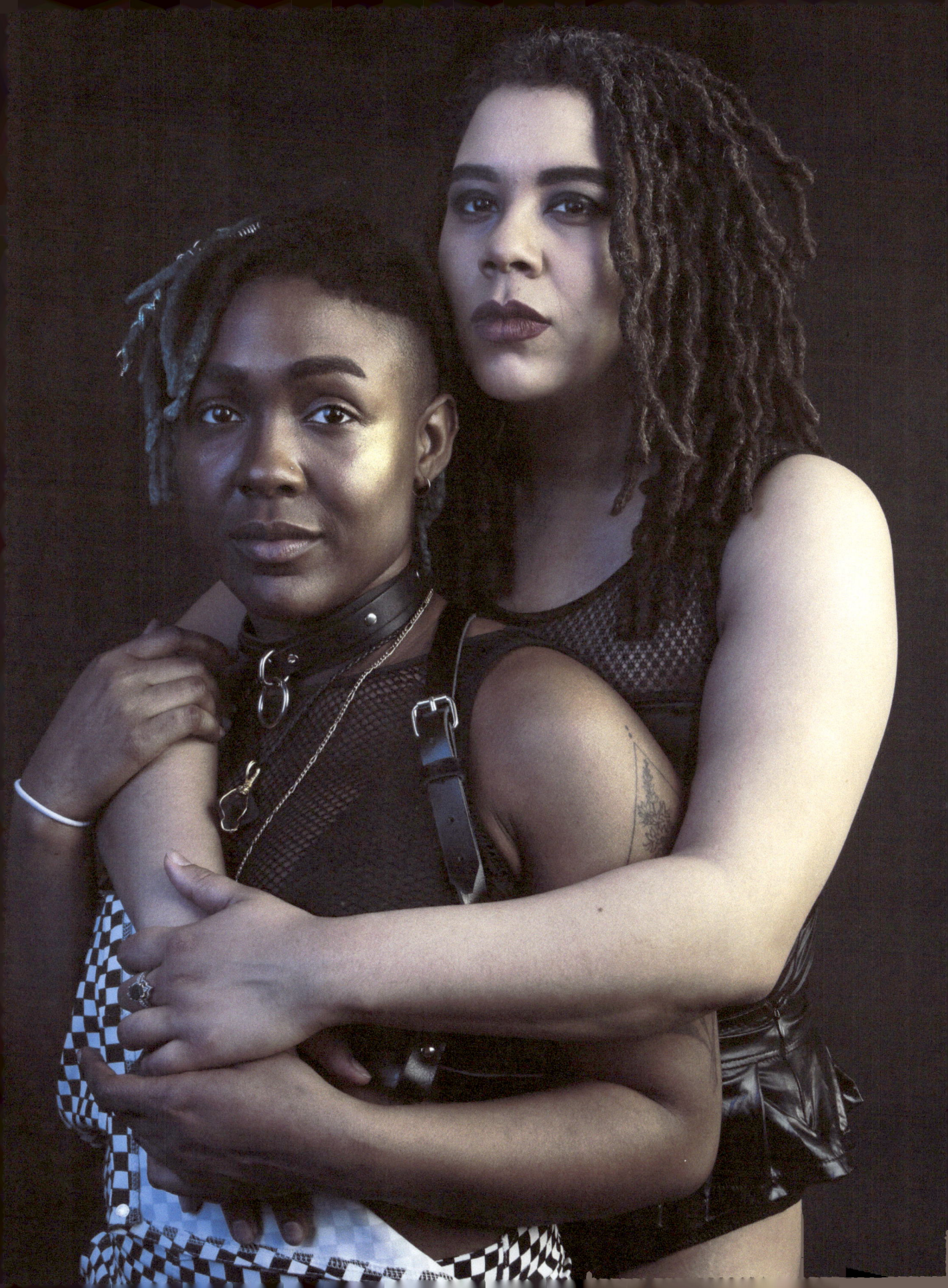

Nastia Gorodilova

Working full-time in the sexual violence field, I rarely make dedicated space anymore to sit still with my experiences, think about how they have changed me, and channel that energy into a feeling of empowerment. Participating in this project has allowed me to center and celebrate my narrative and transformations. Five years on, I wanted to explore the impact that violence has had on my passions and career, my understanding of power and gender, and my concepts of forgiveness, accountability, and justice.

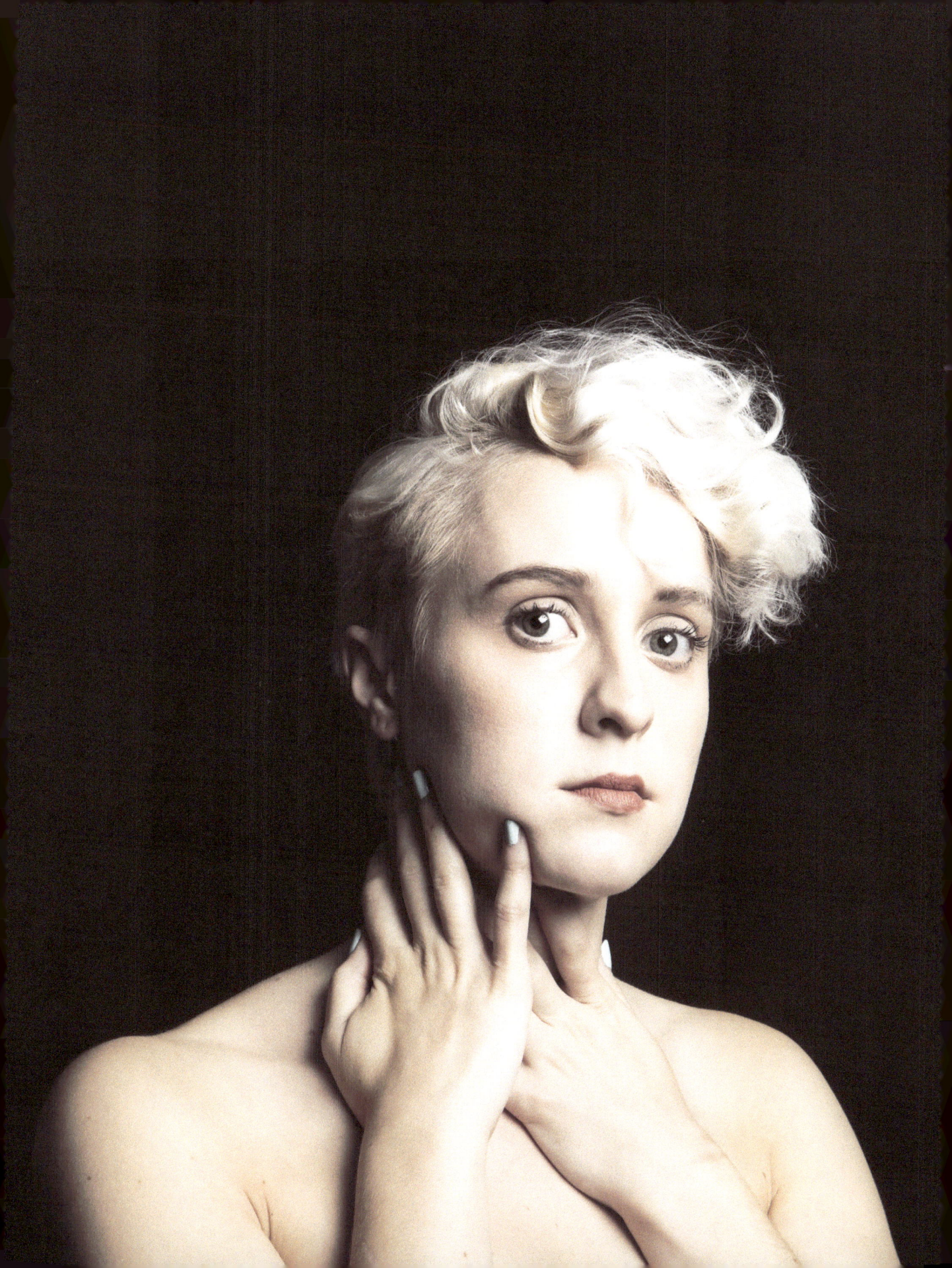

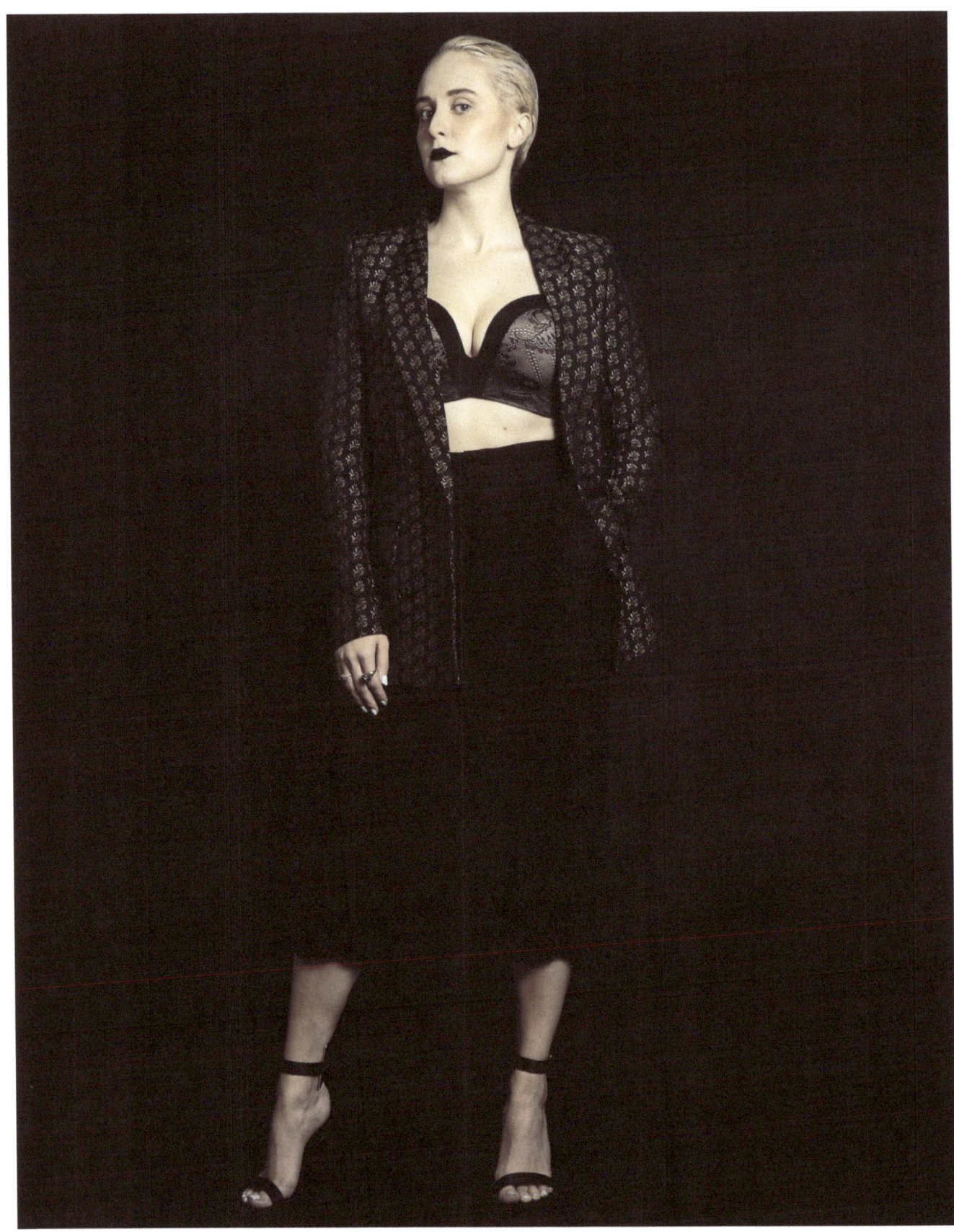

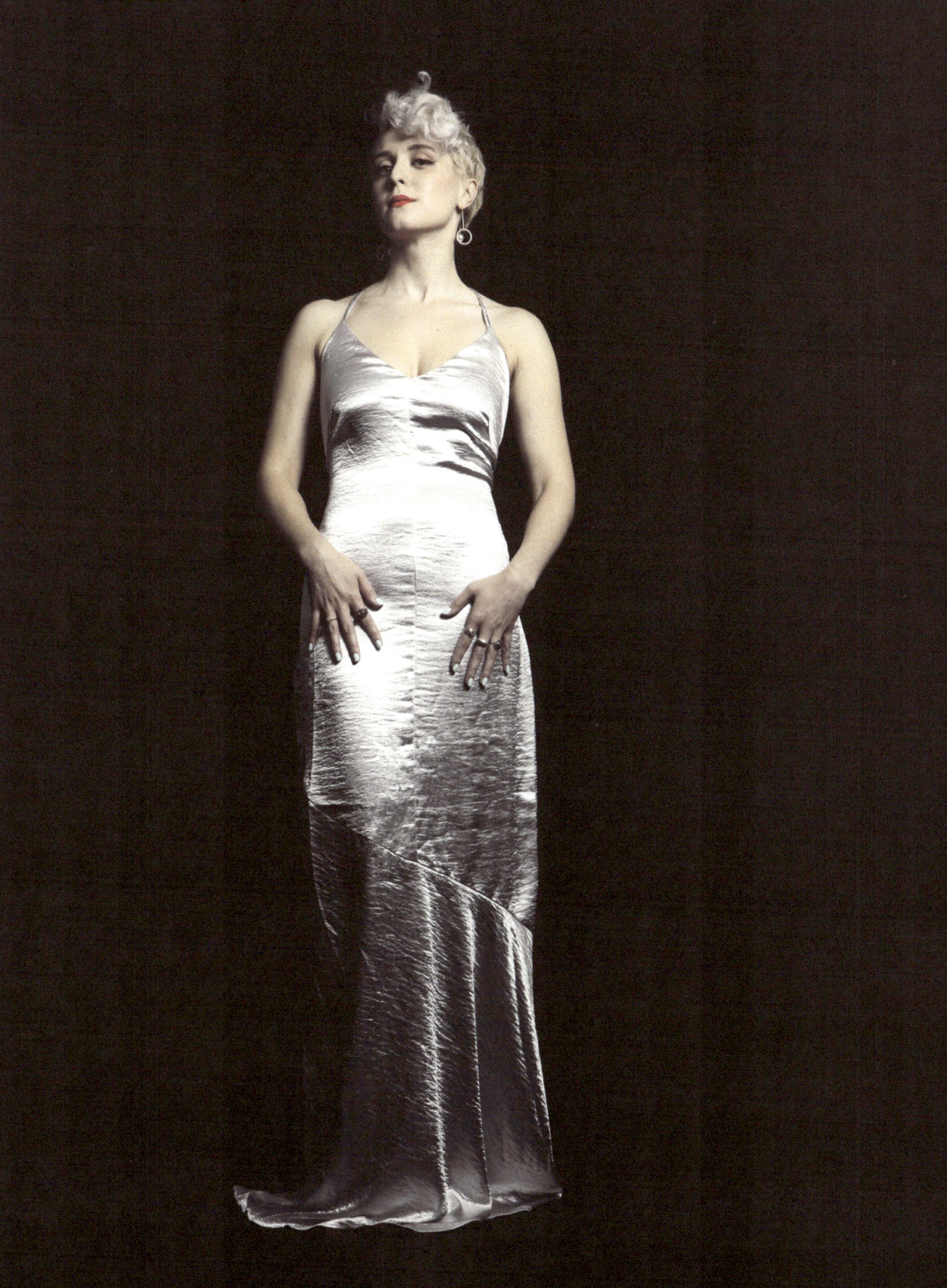

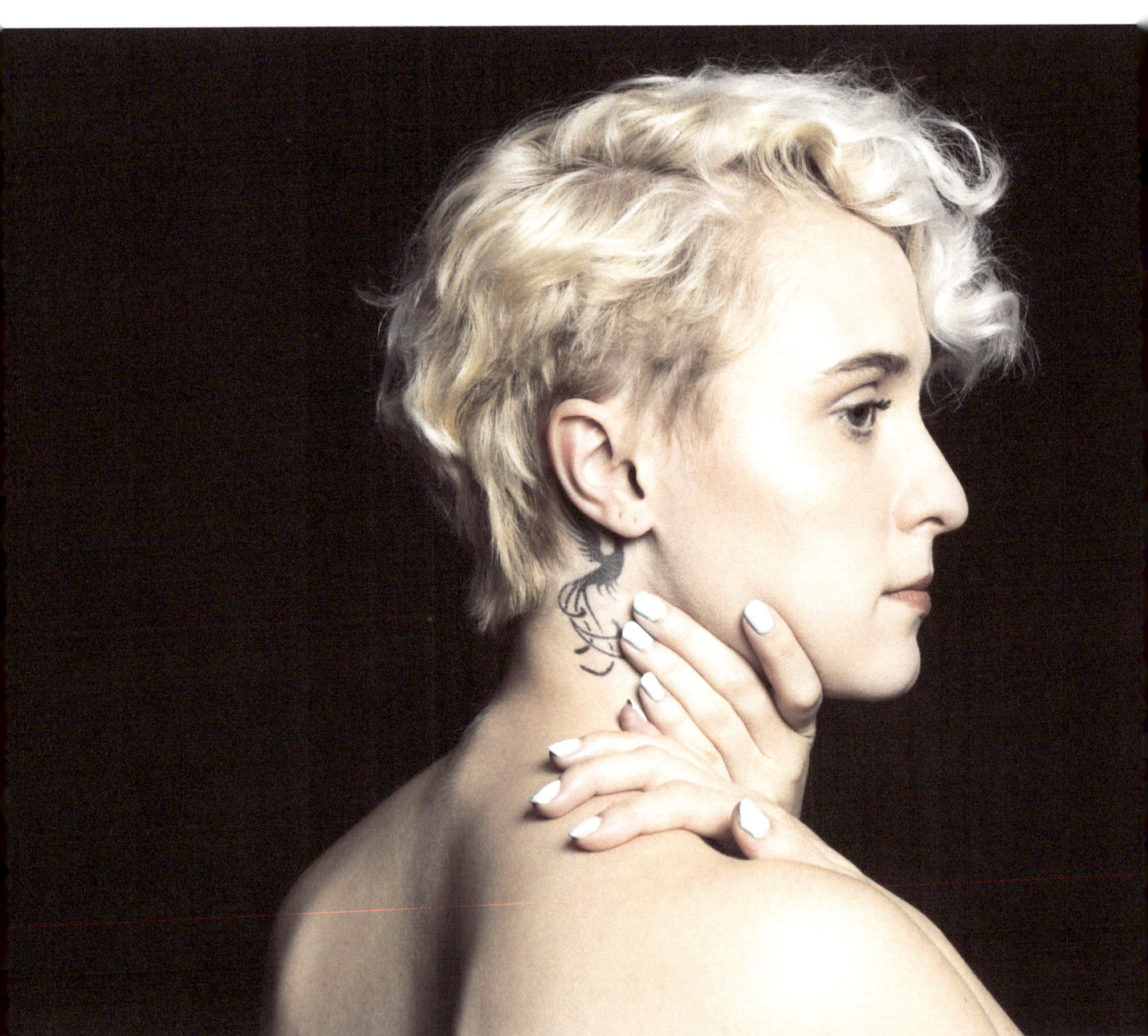

TRANSFORMATION

: an induced or spontaneous thorough & significant change

I believe that my transformation, a thorough & lifelong change of my identities, can be beautiful — even if induced by another & sourced from harm.

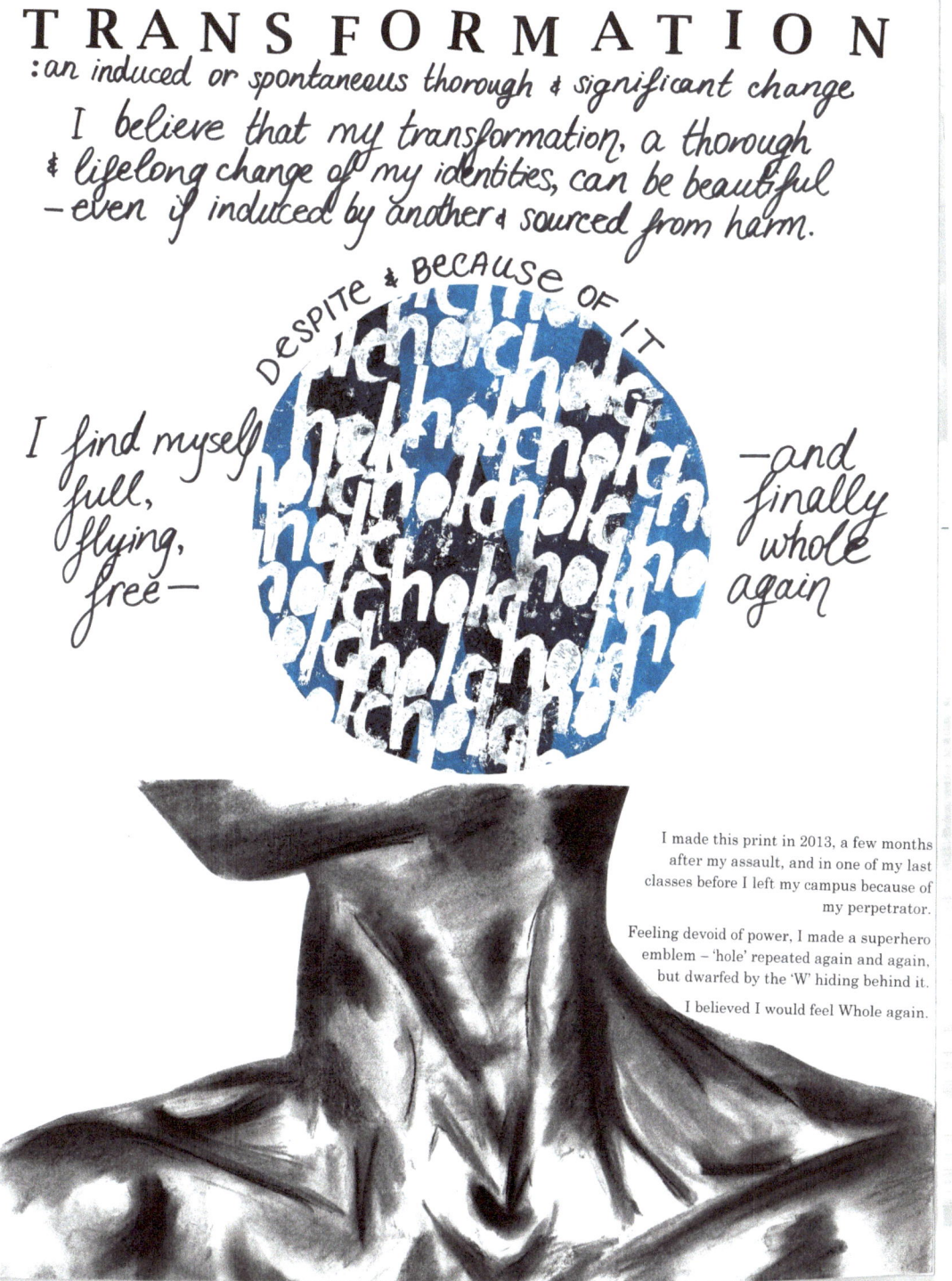

DESPITE & BECAUSE OF IT

I find myself full, flying, free—

—and finally whole again

I made this print in 2013, a few months after my assault, and in one of my last classes before I left my campus because of my perpetrator.

Feeling devoid of power, I made a superhero emblem – 'hole' repeated again and again, but dwarfed by the 'W' hiding behind it.

I believed I would feel Whole again.

www.ingramcontent.com/pod-product-compliance
Lightning Source LLC
Chambersburg PA
CBHW051212220526
45473CB00003B/1005